New Directions for Student Leadership

Susan R. Komives
EDITOR-IN-CHIEF

Kathy L. Guthrie
ASSOCIATE EDITOR

A Competency-Based Approach for Student Leadership Development

Corey Seemiller

Number 156 • Winter 2017
Jossey-Bass
San Francisco

A Competency-Based Approach for Student Leadership Development
Corey Seemiller (ed.)
New Directions for Student Leadership, No. 156, Winter 2017

Editor-in-Chief: *Susan R. Komives*
Associate Editor: *Kathy L. Guthrie*

NEW DIRECTIONS FOR STUDENT LEADERSHIP, (Print ISSN: 2373-3349; Online ISSN: 2373-3357), is published quarterly by Wiley Subscription Services, Inc., a Wiley Company, 111 River St., Hoboken, NJ 07030-5774 USA.

Postmaster: Send all address changes to NEW DIRECTIONS FOR STUDENT LEADERSHIP, John Wiley & Sons Inc., C/O The Sheridan Press, PO Box 465, Hanover, PA 17331 USA.

Information for subscribers
New Directions for Student Leadership is published in 4 issues per year. Institutional subscription prices for 2017 are:
Print & Online: US$462 (US), US$516 (Canada & Mexico), US$562 (Rest of World), €366 (Europe), £290 (UK). Prices are exclusive of tax. Asia-Pacific G ST, C anadian G ST/HST a nd E uropean V AT w ill b e a pplied a t t he a ppropriate r ates. F or m ore i nformation on current tax rates, please go to www.wileyonlinelibrary.com/tax-vat. The price includes online access to the current and all online back files t o J anuary 1 st 2 013, w here a vailable. F or o ther p ricing o ptions, i ncluding a ccess i nformation a nd t erms a nd c onditions, p lease visit www.wileyonlinelibrary.com/access.

Delivery Terms and Legal Title
Where the subscription price includes print issues and delivery is to the recipient's address, delivery terms are **Delivered at Place (DAP)**; the recipient is responsible for paying any import duty or taxes. Title to all issues transfers FOB our shipping point, freight prepaid. We will endeavour to fulfil claims for missing or damaged copies within six months of publication, within our reasonable discretion and subject to availability.

Back issues: Single issues from current and recent volumes are available at the current single issue price from cs-journals@wiley.com.

Disclaimer
The Publisher and Editors cannot be held responsible for errors or any consequences arising from the use of information contained in this journal; the views and opinions expressed do not necessarily reflect those of the Publisher and Editors, neither does the publication of advertisements constitute any endorsement by the Publisher and Editors of the products advertised.

Publisher: New Directions for Student Leadership is published by Wiley Periodicals, Inc., 350 Main St., Malden, MA 02148-5020.

Journal Customer Services: For ordering information, claims and any enquiry concerning your journal subscription please go to www.wileycustomerhelp.com/ask or contact your nearest office.
Americas: Email: cs-journals@wiley.com; Tel: +1 781 388 8598 or +1 800 835 6770 (toll free in the USA & Canada).
Europe, Middle East and Africa: Email: cs-journals@wiley.com; Tel: +44 (0) 1865 778315.
Asia Pacific: E mail: cs-journals@wiley.com; Tel: +65 6511 8000.
Japan: For Japanese speaking support, Email: cs-japan@wiley.com.
Visit our Online Customer Help available in 7 languages at www.wileycustomerhelp.com/ask

Production Editor: Meghanjali Singh (email: mesingh@wiley.com).

Wiley's Corporate Citizenship initiative seeks to address the environmental, social, economic, and ethical challenges faced in our business and which are important to our diverse stakeholder groups. Since launching the initiative, we have focused on sharing our content with those in need, enhancing community philanthropy, reducing our carbon impact, creating global guidelines and best practices for paper use, establishing a vendor code of ethics, and engaging our colleagues and other stakeholders in our efforts. Follow our progress at www.wiley.com/go/citizenship

View this journal online at wileyonlinelibrary.com/journal/yd

Wiley is a founding member of the UN-backed HINARI, AGORA, and OARE initiatives. They are now collectively known as Research4Life, making online scientific content available free or at nominal cost to researchers in developing countries. Please visit Wiley's Content Access Corporate Citizenship site: http://www.wiley.com/WileyCDA/Section/id-390082.html

Address for Editorial Correspondence: Associate Editor, Kathy L. Guthrie, *New Directions for Student Leadership*, Email: kguthrie@fsu.edu.

Abstracting and Indexing Services
The Journal is indexed by Academic Search (EBSCO Publishing); Academic Search Alumni Edition (EBSCO Publishing); Academic Search Premier (EBSCO Publishing); Environmental Sciences & Pollution Management (ProQuest); ERA: Educational Research Abstracts Online (T&F); ERIC: Educational Resources Information Center (CSC); Health & Safety Science Abstracts (ProQuest); MEDLINE/PubMed (NLM); Pollution Abstracts (ProQuest); Professional Development Collection (EBSCO Publishing); PsycINFO/Psychological Abstracts (APA); Safety Science & Risk Abstracts (ProQuest); SocINDEX (EBSCO Publishing); Studies on Women & Gender Abstracts (T&F).

Cover design: Wiley
Cover Images: © Lava 4 images | Shutterstock

For submission instructions, subscription and all other information visit:
wileyonlinelibrary.com/journal/yd

Contents

Editor's Notes

Whether addressing environmental problems, human rights issues, international conflict, or the economy, the world needs leaders who can thrive in a time of uncertainty and complexity. Yet, we continue to see examples of unethical and even incompetent leaders who have either not addressed these issues or are contributing to their continued existence. This has led to what appears to be a crisis of leadership facing the world today. Schools, communities, organizations, and workplaces have a vested interest in ethical, competent leadership; in many ways, our lives depend on it. Thus, it is no surprise that there is an abundance of books, articles, blogs, videos, trainings, speakers, and resources dedicated to the topic—supporting the belief that if we help develop leadership capacity in people early on, we might avoid these scenarios of bad leadership.

Given that the concept of leadership is referenced in many institutional mission statements (Seemiller, 2016) and that 100% of all 97 academic accrediting agencies in the United States require students to obtain proficiency in one or more leadership competencies before graduation (Seemiller, 2013), it is no surprise that there is a focus on developing students as leaders. Many educational institutions offer credit-bearing classes, workshops, co-curricular programs, and developmental experiences focused on leadership, with some colleges and universities even offering entire graduate and undergraduate programs in leadership. These opportunities are often aimed at helping students develop the competencies essential for engaging in leadership in their workplaces and communities.

But the task of developing students' leadership competencies can be both elusive and challenging. What competencies are the most critical for students to develop? How can we ensure students are ready to develop leadership competencies? What instructional strategies and program design elements can we use to foster development effectively? How do we help students and educators track and measure competency learning and growth? This issue includes insights from a variety of scholars who attempt to tackle these questions, offering their diverse perspectives and nuanced expertise on: (a) the historical development and current use of leadership competencies in the workforce and in developing college student leaders; (b) the optimal levels of self-efficacy for students to maximize their learning and use of leadership competencies; (c) connecting leadership competency development with Gallup strengths in order to help students develop specific competencies to leverage their talents into strengths;

NEW DIRECTIONS FOR STUDENT LEADERSHIP, no. 156, Winter 2017 © 2017 Wiley Periodicals, Inc., A Wiley Company
Published online in Wiley Online Library (wileyonlinelibrary.com) • DOI: 10.1002/yd.20266

(d) instructional strategies for intentional competency development; (e) the connection between emotional and social intelligence competencies and career readiness, including curricular ideas for on-line learning; (f) designing competency-based leadership programs using elements of gamification; (g) strategies and processes for measuring leadership competency development, including practical ideas for implementation; and (h) integrating a campus-wide leadership competency development approach.

Although the use of competencies has a rich history in organizations, the use of leadership competencies with college students is only in its infancy. But, as funding becomes scarcer and students become more discretionary with their time, using a leadership competency approach can offer institutions quantifiable data to prove the value of leadership development to students, parents, employers, alumni, donors, and institutional administrators. And leadership competencies might just provide the roadmap we need to develop the ethical and competent leaders we need in our world today.

Corey Seemiller
Editor

References

Seemiller, C. (2013). *The student leadership competencies guidebook.* San Francisco, CA: Jossey-Bass.
Seemiller, C. (2016). Leadership competency development: A higher education responsibility. *New Directions for Higher Education, 174,* 93–104.

COREY SEEMILLER *serves as a faculty member in the Department of Leadership Studies in Education and Organizations at Wright State University, teaching undergraduate courses in organizational leadership and graduate courses in leadership development. Dr. Seemiller received her bachelor's degree in communication, master's degree in educational leadership, and Ph.D. in higher education. She is the author of The Student Leadership Competencies Guidebook and associated tools to help educators develop intentional curriculum that enhances leadership competency development, and Generation Z Goes to College, which aims to prepare college educators to serve and develop Generation Z students.*

1   *This chapter provides an overview of leadership competencies including the history of emergence, contemporary uses, common frameworks, challenges, benefits, and future implications.*

Developing Leadership Competencies

Lucy Croft, Corey Seemiller

Are leaders born or made? This is the classic question often posed to students in leadership classes as they grapple with whether they believe the capacity to lead effectively is something that is innate or something that can be learned. Many leadership scholars, however, have asserted there are elements of leadership that can be taught and developed (Zimmerman-Oster & Burkhardt, 2001) through experience, training, classes, or workshops, either separately or through a combination of opportunities (Astin & Astin, 2000; Roberts, 2003). So, what exactly is being taught and developed to help people engage in effective leadership? This chapter will cover the history and emergence of leadership competencies, the use of leadership competencies today, using competencies for college student leadership development, and examples of leadership competencies in action.

History and Emergence of Leadership Competencies

In the late 1960s and early 1970s, a paradigm shift occurred in the field of personnel management from a traditional standard performance approach, centered on individuals' formal qualifications and experiences as predictors of job achievement, to an approach acknowledging greater self-directed behavior and responsibility of the employee in their achievement of job excellence (Horton, Hondeghen, & Farnham, 2002). One way to address this shift was through the use of competencies. Hirsch and Stabler (1995; in Horton et al., 2002) "define competencies as the skills, knowledge, experience, attributes and behavior that an individual needs to perform a job effectively" (p. 4).

Using competencies in a job setting, often referred to as competency-based management, involves identifying the varied knowledge, values, abilities, and behaviors that people need to possess and exercise to achieve the strategic objectives, goals, and performance expectations of the

NEW DIRECTIONS FOR STUDENT LEADERSHIP, no. 156, Winter 2017 © 2017 Wiley Periodicals, Inc., A Wiley Company
Published online in Wiley Online Library (wileyonlinelibrary.com) • DOI: 10.1002/yd.20267

organization. Competency-based management can provide a framework for recruitment (What competencies should be in this job description and how do I market to prospective employees who have those competencies?); selection (Which prospective candidate best possesses the competencies necessary for the job?); training (How can I create training experiences that help develop the competencies associated with the position?); and the development of incentives, recognitions, and rewards (What can I do to recognize the development and achievement of essential competencies?) (Horton et al., 2002).

The work of psychologist David McClelland is associated with developing the modern concept of competencies (German & Johnson, 2006). McClelland (1973) reviewed with some skepticism the main lines of evidence for the validity of intelligence and aptitude tests through standardized testing. Disillusioned with the idea that test achievement could be the only determination to qualify a person for admittance into schools or colleges or for employment purposes, McClelland offered alternatives to traditional intelligence testing. The alternatives concentrated on the analysis of the behavior of a person, the changes reflected based on the learning acquired, and the consideration of various situations in which the person is critiqued (McClelland).

Additionally, McClelland (1973) asserted that testing for personality variables or competencies of life outcomes such as communication skills, patience, moderate goal setting, and ego development (taking initiative), could be a strong indicator of one's abilities. His principles for defining a new alternative testing analysis method were centered as much on evaluating educational progress as they were in identifying fixed characteristics for selection purposes into schools, employment, or advancement (McClelland).

McClelland's approach has provided an important foundation for shaping the modern definition of personal competencies and traction for the competency movement. In the early 1980s, the American Management Association conducted a study in which competencies were defined as "underlying characteristics of an individual that is causally related to effective or superior performance in a job" (Boyatzis, 1982, p. 21). By the late 1990s and early 2000s, it became increasingly clear that many jobs in the modern workplace required some level of leadership aptitude (Bolden & Gosling, 2006). "Leadership competencies shifted emphasis from the mainly technical requirements of specific jobs to the softer interpersonal qualities sought from people at many levels across an organization" (Bolden & Gosling, 2006, p. 5).

Leadership Competencies Today

Both the Society for Human Resource Management and the United States Office of Personnel Management promote the use of leadership competencies in the workplace. The Society for Human Resource Management (2008) defines leadership competencies as "leadership skills and behaviors that contribute to superior performance" (p. 1), whereas the Office of Personnel Management (n.d.) defines a competency as "a measurable pattern of knowledge, skills, abilities, behaviors, and other characteristics that an individual needs to perform work roles or occupational functions successfully" (para. 1). Leadership competencies can be found in corporate settings and professional associations across a multitude of fields.

Corporate Leadership Competencies.   Today, many companies use leadership competencies for training, development, and evaluation. The Walt Disney Company, through the Disney Institute, provides training and instruction on three core competencies: leadership, employee engagement, and service. These core competencies reflect their business approach to customer service and leadership (Disney, n.d.). The Microsoft Corporation focuses on four key skills for training and development: values-based leadership practices, communication skills, specific business strategies and financial comprehension, and insights in leading at the enterprise level (Bluepoint Leadership Development, n.d.).

Professional Association Leadership Competencies.   In addition to the use of competencies in specific workplaces, leadership competencies are also used in professional associations to provide a foundation for effective professional performance. For example, the Public Relations Society of America requires their professionals to acquire knowledge, skills, and abilities in the following areas: researching, planning, implementing and evaluating programs, leading the public relations function, managing relationships, applying ethics and law, managing issues and crisis communications, understanding communication models, and theories and history of the profession (Universal Accreditation Board, 2016).

In the accounting profession, the American Institute of Certified Public Accountants (AICPA) defines a set of skill-based competencies necessary for those looking to enter the field of accounting. The core personal competencies essential for the accounting professional include professional demeanor, problem-solving and decision-making, interaction, leadership, communication, project management, and leveraging technology to develop and enhance personal competencies (American Institute of CPAs, 2016).

Student Affairs Leadership Competencies.   Student Affairs professionals, who serve in roles focused on college student development and student life, are also well versed in professional development and skill-based achievement through competency development. NASPA: Student Affairs Administrators in Higher Education and ACPA: College Student Educators International joined forces to create the Professional Competency Areas for the Student Affairs Practitioners to define the broad professional "knowledge, skills and in some cases, attitudes expected of student affairs professionals" (ACPA & NASPA, 2015, p. 6). The following are the

NEW DIRECTIONS FOR STUDENT LEADERSHIP • DOI: 10.1002/yd

professional competency areas for student affairs educators: personal and ethical foundations; values, philosophy, and history; assessment, evaluation, and research; law, policy, and governance; organizational and human resource; leadership; social justice and inclusion; student learning and development; technology; and advising and supporting (ACPA & NASPA, 2015).

National Leadership Education Research Agenda Leadership Competencies.   There are also core competencies aimed at leadership educators more specifically. The National Leadership Education Research Agenda (NLERA) released in 2013 established seven priorities vital for leadership education (Andenoro, 2013). The first two priorities, in particular, fall under Pedagogical Priorities—The Applied How of Leadership Education. These priorities focus on "leadership learning and transfer of learning through innovative leadership education" and include the critical practices of teaching, learning, and curriculum development, as well as program assessment and evaluation (Andenoro, 2013, p. 3).

In addition, one of the standards of the Council for the Advancement of Standards in Higher Education (2012) is for Student Leadership Programs. It outlines 10 competencies essential for leadership educators, including diversity, communication, reflection, and group dynamics.

Using Competencies for College Student Leadership Development

Given the widespread use of competencies in the professional sector, colleges and universities provide an ideal environment for helping students develop leadership competencies before they enter their future careers (Seemiller, 2016a). Thus, identifying critical competencies for students to develop is a key piece of leadership program design. The W.K. Kellogg Foundation identified four categories for an exemplary leadership program, which include competencies such as problem solving and self-assessment embedded into the framework (Zimmerman-Oster & Burkhardt, 2001). Described in more detail below, other frameworks focused more specifically on leadership competency development for students include the National Association for Campus Activities (NACA) competencies (Brill et al., 2009), Student Leadership Competencies (Seemiller, 2013b), the Five Practices of Exemplary Leadership (Kouzes & Posner, 1987), and the National Association for Colleges and Employers (NACE) Career Readiness Competencies (2014).

NACA Competencies.   Acknowledging the necessity for identifying leadership competencies for college students, the NACA Education Advisory group, comprised of student affairs professionals throughout the United States, developed The Competency Guide for College Student Leaders. This guide serves as a "learning map for student leaders as they grow and develop through participation in student organizations, community service, campus employment, grassroots activities, leadership positions, followership positions, mentoring relationships with campus activities advisors, etc." (Brill et al., 2009, p. 2). The resource highlights 10 core competencies from the Council for the Advancement of Standards in Higher Education related to working with students (Brill et al., 2009). These competencies include leadership development, assessment and evaluation, event management, meaningful interpersonal relationships, collaboration, social responsibility, effective communication, multicultural competency, intellectual growth, and clarified values (Brill et al., 2009). NACA also offers a facilitator guide and evaluation instrument based on these competencies.

Student Leadership Competencies.   Based on more than 5 years of extensive research, The Student Leadership Competencies Guidebook includes 60 leadership competencies for the twenty-first century (Seemiller, 2013b). This list of competencies emerged through an analysis of components of three contemporary leadership models, content from the 2006 CAS Standards (Council for the Advancement of Standards in Higher Education, 2006) and ACPA and NASPA's 2004 Learning Reconsidered document (Day et al., 2004), as well as nearly 18,000 learning outcomes embedded into the accreditation manuals of all 522 accredited academic programs in U.S. higher education. These 60 leadership competencies are categorized in eight clusters: learning and reasoning, self-awareness and development, interpersonal interaction, group dynamics, civic responsibility, communication, strategic planning, and personal behavior (Seemiller, 2013b). Further, each competency includes four dimensions that reflect levels of learning. These include the knowledge (content), value (belief), ability (skill or motivation), and behavior (action).

The Student Leadership Competencies Guidebook (Seemiller, 2013b) serves as a framework to develop a program or course, infuse meaningful competency-based activities into the curriculum, and help students reflect and apply their learning in future academic, professional, and life contexts (Seemiller, 2013b). Educators can also utilize the Student Leadership Competencies to assess competency learning and development using various tools such as the online inventory, evaluation measurements, and rubrics, as well as award digital leadership competency badges to recognize student achievement.

Five Practices of Exemplary Leadership.   In 1987, Kouzes and Posner published The Leadership Challenge, which presented five practices of exemplary leadership. The practices, model the way, challenge the process, enable others to act, inspire a shared vision, and encourage the heart (Kouzes & Posner, 1987), are grounded in decades of research (Kouzes & Posner, 2017). Each of the five practices is comprised of a multitude of individual competencies, which can be found on the Jossey-Bass Student Leadership Competencies Database website (Seemiller, 2013a).

The five practices of exemplary leadership were later linked to high school and college student populations, resulting in the creation of The Student Leadership Challenge (Kouzes & Posner, 2008) and a student version of the Leadership Practices Inventory called the Student Leadership Practices Inventory (Kouzes & Posner, 1998). This inventory marked one of the earlier adopted skill-based inventories for assessing one's competencies for leading. The Student Leadership Practices Inventory (Student LPI) is designed to assess students' areas of strength as well as areas warranting further development in the five areas of practice. The authors assert that "the more frequently students are perceived as engaging in the behavior and actions identified in the Student LPI, the more likely it is that students will be perceived as effective leaders" (Kouzes & Posner, 1998, p. 7). The Student LPI consists of both the student's self-assessment of their behaviors around the five practices and an observer's external assessment. Once both parties have completed their assessments independently, responses are cross-referenced to identify the consistencies and inconsistencies focusing on students' strengths and areas of improvement.

NACE Career Readiness Competencies.   The National Association for Colleges and Employers (NACE) has also established key leadership competencies for career readiness. In 2014, a task force of career services and HR professionals conducted a study of 606 employers (NACE, 2014) and determined seven competencies essential for being hired in the workforce. These include critical thinking/problem solving, oral/written communications, teamwork/collaboration, information technology application, leadership, professionalism/work ethic, and career management (NACE, n.d.). To put these competencies into practices, NACE offers resources such as evaluation forms, a resume rubric, and links to course syllabi and program descriptions using the NACE career readiness competencies.

Examples of Leadership Competencies in Action

In addition to providing the frameworks and resources related to leadership competencies, it is also important to highlight tangible examples of using leadership competencies with students. These examples are offered to provoke additional interest in learning more about leadership competencies and to showcase their wide variety of use.

Co-Curricular Leadership Programs.   The Geneseo Opportunities for Leadership Development (GOLD) Program at the State University of New York (SUNY) at Geneseo "seeks to prepare students for college and community leadership roles and responsibilities in service to the college and the global community" (Matthews, 2013, p. 17). This mission is delivered through a comprehensive educational, developmental, and training series of workshops, volunteer work, and active engagement. A comprehensive overview of the program and workshop modules can be found in Building Leaders One Hour at a Time: Guidebook for Leadership Development (Matthews, 2013). The Student Leadership Competencies Implementation Handbook (Seemiller, 2016b) identifies the specific competencies associated with each workshop module so educators can easily find a module that addresses the intended competency.

Another example of a co-curricular leadership program that uses competencies is the Advanced Leadership Challenge at Florida International University. In this program, students participate in one distinct leadership experience (such as a workshop, event, role) from each of the eight Student Leadership Competencies clusters (Seemiller, 2013b). After completing a reflection on the experience, students are awarded a leadership medallion to wear at graduation (Florida International University, 2016).

Experiential Learning Transcripts.   The University of North Florida offers a Leadership Certificate Program, which consists of 15 academic credit hours and requires students to create an Experiential Learning Transcript. Through reflective practice, the Experiential Learning Transcript enables the student to identify leadership competencies they developed through various activities including employment, community service, study and travel abroad, internships, and engagement in campus and community organizations and projects (University of North Florida, n.d.).

Student Leadership Conferences.   In fall 2015, Lead365 entered the leadership education and development arena as a competency-based national student leadership conference. The conference curriculum aligns with three developmental progressions of a leader: engage, explore, and evolve, with each level focusing on a specific set of leadership competencies.

- Explore: Enhancing inspiration for self-awareness, understanding leadership, building personal leadership abilities and skill sets, and identifying a mission and leadership purpose
- Engage: Developing interpersonal communication competencies and creating environments for collaboration and teamwork
- Evolve: Understanding social justice and diversity, facilitating change, and embracing social responsibility

Each conference session is mapped to both a developmental level and a specific leadership competency. Students are able to select sessions to attend based on competencies they would like to develop, making the conference experience more intentionally developmental. Although the sessions to choose from are diverse in terms of competency focus, the 2016 conference also offered students an opportunity to hone in on one specific competency to engage in deep learning and development. Students who selected and participated in eight workshops and leadership labs related to the competency of verbal communication were able to earn a Student Leadership Competencies digital badge in Verbal Communication to showcase on social media and in their ePortfolios (Lead365, 2016).

Academic Leadership Programs.   In addition to the co-curriculum, leadership competencies can also be used in credit-bearing leadership programs. For example, Wright State University has mapped each course in the undergraduate Organizational Leadership major to specific leadership competencies (B. Kraner, personal communication, January 3, 2017). By identifying the competencies connected with each required course, the faculty members could make curricular modifications to address additional competencies as needed, generate marketing ideas around the intended competencies, develop an ePortfolio requirement for students that aligns with the selected competencies, and assess student competency development through end-of-semester evaluations.

Self-Evaluations.   In recent years, there has been increased attention to performance-based accountability in higher education, especially in employability upon graduation (Peck et al., 2015; Seemiller, 2013b). This has led to the creation of NACA® NEXT (NACA, 2015), which is designed to assist students as they prepare for their career aspirations upon graduation. NACA® NEXT offers a self-evaluation tool based on NACE survey results of the skills employers seek. Students also have the option of inviting their advisor or activities professional to evaluate them on these same skills so that the students can compare their self-evaluation with evaluations from professionals and peers. The evaluation also includes recommendations for students to enhance their skills through leadership activities and engagement.

Another self-evaluation tool available to students is the Student Leadership Competencies Inventory (Seemiller, 2016c). The online inventory is comprised of eight mini-inventories. Each includes measurements that assess competency proficiency (ability to enact a competency) for each competency in that cluster. For example, the Communication mini-inventory measures competencies such as Verbal Communication and Listening. Upon completion of each mini-inventory, a report is generated showcasing how students self-report their competency proficiency. For those who want more of a comparison tool, the Student Leadership Competencies 360 evaluation allows students to complete a self-evaluation of their competency performance (effective use of a competency) across all 60 competencies and compare it with evaluations completed by observers, which can include supervisors, advisors, instructors, and peers.

Professional Development.   In 2014, the topic of the National Leadership Symposium hosted by the National Clearinghouse for Leadership Programs (NCLP) and NACA was "Leadership Competencies from Research to Results." During the symposium, several scholars and practitioners came together to discuss strategies to integrate leadership competency development and measurement in their programs and courses. Each participant was given a copy of The Student Leadership Competencies Guidebook (Seemiller, 2013b) as a resource and was asked to work in small groups to develop a project that included competency setting, curriculum development, facilitation, and assessment.

Challenges and Benefits in Using Leadership Competencies with Students

It is important to note some challenges in using leadership competencies with students. First, leadership competency models tend to focus on individual skill development (leader development) and less on collaboration and relationship-oriented approaches (leadership development). Bolden and Gosling (2006) state, "competency frameworks tend to reinforce individualistic practices that dissociate leaders from the relational environment in which they operate and could, arguably, inhibit the emergence of more inclusive and collective forms of leadership" (p. 13). Therefore, it is important to remain mindful of context and relationships within leadership situations and to help students learn how to leverage their own competencies along with the competencies of others for effective group functioning. Although this issue focuses on individual development, future research may explore how groups and communities develop collective competencies. The Social Change Model of Leadership Development, for example, offers three levels of development: individual, group, and community (Higher Education Research Institute, 1996), in which competency development at the group and community levels may be useful both for the process and outcome of leadership.

In addition, certain challenges arise through the wide variation of competency models that exist. Models with a large number of competencies might suggest it is not possible to develop all competencies, thus creating a sense of feeling overwhelmed with choices. On the other hand, some models may have too few competencies that do not reflect the true complexity of leadership (Hollenbeck, McCall, & Silzer, 2006).

Although there can be challenges, there are benefits in utilizing leadership competencies with students. First, leadership competencies can provide a theoretical foundation from which to build programs, courses, and experiences for leadership education. Second, using a common competency language can help create bridges between student affairs and academic units (for marketing, partnership, and accreditation purposes) as well as give students the language to use with prospective employers. Finally, as leadership development may be elusive to measure, there are many tools specifically designed to measure leadership competency development. Having an assessment protocol and set of tools around leadership competency development can create a systematic way to gather data that can be used in annual reports, marketing materials, and to seek performance-based funding.

Conclusion

It is evident that leadership programs have the opportunity to benefit students' undergraduate experience directly, as they provide a "sense of integration in the collegiate experience, higher rates of retention, and a stronger sense of involvement in the surrounding community" (Zimmerman-Oster & Burkhardt, 2001, p. 67). Utilizing a leadership competency-based approach can provide an intentional and developmental way to design programs, develop curriculum, conduct assessment, and recognize learning for deep and meaningful student leadership development.

References

ACPA: College Student Educators International, & NASPA—Student Affairs Administrators in Higher Education. (2015). *ACPA/NASPA professional competency areas for student affairs practitioners*. Washington, DC: Authors.

American Institute of CPAs. (2016). *Core competency framework*. Retrieved from https://www.aicpa.org/InterestAreas/AccountingEducation/Resources/Pages/Core Competency.aspx

Andenoro, A. C. (2013). The national leadership education research agenda: Strategic priorities and deepened perspectives. *Journal of Leadership Education, 12*(3), 1–9.

Astin, A. W., & Astin, H. S. (2000). *Leadership reconsidered*. Battle Creek, MI: W. K. Kellogg Foundation.

Bluepoint Leadership Development. (n.d.). *Microsoft*. Retrieved from http://www.blue pointleadership.com/client/microsoft/

Bolden, R., & Gosling, J. (2006). Leadership competencies: Time to change the tune? *Leadership, 2*, 147–163.

Boyatzis, R. E. (1982). *The competent manager*. New York, NY: John Wiley and Sons, Inc.

Brill, K., Croft, L., Ogle, J., Russell, S., Smedick, B., Hicks, M., & Coats, S. (2009). *Competency guide for college student leaders*. Columbia, SC: NACA.

Council for the Advancement of Standards in Higher Education. (2006). *CAS professional standards for higher education* (6th ed.). Washington, DC: Author.

Day, P., Dungy, G. J., Fried, J., Komives, S. R., McDonald, W. M., & Salvador, S. (2004). *Learning reconsidered: A campus-wide focus on the student experience*. Washington, DC: National Association of Student Personnel Administrators and American College Personnel Association.

Disney. (n.d.). *Our story*. Retrieved from https://disneyinstitute.com/about/our-story/

Florida International University. (2016). *Advanced leadership challenge*. Retrieved from http://studentaffairs.fiu.edu/get-involved/leadership-and-service/graduation-medals/ advanced-leadership-challenge/index.php

German, A. N., & Johnson, M. P. (2006). Leadership competencies: An introduction. *Journal of Health Care Management, 51*, 7–13.

Higher Education Research Institute. (1996). *A social change model of leadership development: Guidebook version III*. College Park, MD: National Clearinghouse for Leadership Programs.

Hollenbeck, G. P., McCall, M. W., Jr., & Silzer, R. F. (2006). Leadership competency models. *The Leadership Quarterly, 17*, 398–413.

Horton, S., Hondeghen, A., & Farnham, D. (2002). *Competency management in the public sector: European variations on a theme*. Amsterdam, Netherlands: IOP Press.

Kouzes, J. M., & Posner, B. Z. (1987). *The leadership challenge* (1st ed.). San Francisco, CA: Jossey-Bass.

Kouzes, J. M., & Posner, B. Z. (1998). *Student leadership practices inventory*. San Francisco, CA: Jossey-Bass.

Kouzes, J. M., & Posner, B. Z. (2008). *Student leadership challenge* (1st ed.). San Francisco, CA: Jossey-Bass.

Kouzes, J. M., & Posner, B. Z. (2017). *Our authors' research*. Retrieved from http://www.leadershipchallenge.com/research-section-our-authors-research.aspx

Lead365. (2016). *Curriculum*. Retrieved from http://www.lead365.org/national-conference/curriculum/

Matthews, T. (2013). *Building leaders one hour at a time: Guidebook for leadership development*. East Rochester, NY: CJM Books.

McClelland, D. C. (1973). Testing for "competence" rather than intelligence. *American Psychologist, 28*, 1–14.

National Association for Campus Activities (NACA). (2015). *NACA next*. Retrieved from https://www.naca.org/Next/Pages/default.aspx

National Association of Colleges and Employers (NACE). (2014). *Career readiness competencies: Employer survey results*. Retrieved from http://www.naceweb.org/knowledge/career-readiness-employer-survey-results.aspx

National Association of Colleges and Employers (NACE). (n.d.). *Career readiness defined*. Retrieved from http://www.naceweb.org/knowledge/career-readiness-competencies.aspx

Office of Personnel Management. (n.d.). *Assessment and selection: Competencies*. Retrieved from https://www.opm.gov/policy-data-oversight/assessment-and-selection/competencies/

Peck, A., Cramp, C., Croft, L., Cummings, T., Kristal, F., Hall, D., ... Lawhead, J. (2015). *Considering the impact of participation and employment of students in campus activities and collegiate recreation on the development of the skills employers desire most*. NACA and NIRSA [White Paper]. Retrieved from http://nirsa.net/nirsa/wp-content/uploads/NACA_NIRSA_White_Paper.pdf

Roberts, D. C. (2003). Crossing boundaries in leadership program design. In C. Cherrey, J. J. Gardiner, & N. Huber (Eds.), *Building leadership bridges* (pp. 137–149). Sommerville, MA: Emerald.

Seemiller, C. (2013a). *Jossey-Bass student leadership competencies database*. Retrieved from http://www.wiley.com/WileyCDA/Section/id-818224.html

Seemiller, C. (2013b). *The student leadership competencies guidebook*. San Francisco, CA: Jossey-Bass.

Seemiller, C. (2016a). Leadership competency development: A higher education responsibility. *New Directions for Higher Education, 174*, 93–104.

Seemiller, C. (2016b). *Student leadership competencies implementation handbook*. Retrieved from www.studentleadershipcompetencies.com

Seemiller, C. (2016c). *Student leadership competencies inventory*. Retrieved from http://studentleadershipcompetencies.com/tools/inventory/

Society for Human Resource Management. (2008). *Leadership competencies*. Retrieved from https://www.shrm.org/resourcesandtools/hr-topics/behavioral-competencies/leadership-and-navigation/pages/leadershipcompetencies.aspx

Universal Accreditation Board. (2016). *Study guide for the examination for accreditation in public relations* (3rd ed.). Retrieved from www.praccreditation.org

University of North Florida. (n. d.). *Experiential learning transcript (ELT)*. Retrieved from http://www.unf.edu/taylor-leadership/About_ELT.aspx

Zimmerman-Oster, K., & Burkhardt, J. (2001). *Leadership in the making: Impact and insights from leadership development programs in U.S. colleges and universities*. Battle Creek, MI: W. K. Kellogg Foundation.

LUCY CROFT serves as the associate vice president for student affairs and adjunct instructor for the College of Education and Human Services at the University of North Florida as well as the 2017/2018 chair of the Board of Directors for NACA. She holds a doctorate in education with a concentration in curriculum development and instruction emphasizing leadership and higher education administration.

COREY SEEMILLER is a faculty member in the Department of Leadership Studies in Education and Organizations at Wright State University and was formerly the director of Leadership Programs at The University of Arizona. She has served as the co-chair for the National Leadership Symposium and co-chair for the Leadership Education Academy and is the author of The Student Leadership Competencies Guidebook and Generation Z Goes to College.

NEW DIRECTIONS FOR STUDENT LEADERSHIP • DOI: 10.1002/yd

2

This chapter covers the role of students' self-efficacy in developing their leadership competencies. Practical strategies and recommendations are provided.

The Interaction of Efficacy and Leadership Competency Development

Moe Machida-Kosuga

Fostering leadership has long been a primary targeted personal development outcome for students in higher education. Various factors related to leadership competency development have been identified, including environmental factors such as feedback (Van Velsor, McCauley, & Ruderman, 2010), opportunities for challenges (DeRue & Wellman, 2009), social support (Machida, Schaubroeck, & Feltz, 2016), mentoring (Allen, Eby, Poteet, & Lentz, 2004), as well as individual factors such as learning orientation (Dragoni, Tesluck, Russell, & Oh, 2009), readiness (Reichard & Thompson, 2016), and motivation to lead (Chan & Drasgow, 2001). Among these factors, researchers and practitioners have recognized confidence to play a central role in leadership competency development (Hannah, Avolio, Luthans, & Harms, 2008; Machida & Schaubroeck, 2011).

Confidence, or self-efficacy, to use a social psychology term, can be defined as "beliefs in one's capabilities to organize and execute the courses of action required to produce a given attainment" (Bandura, 1997, p. 3). Researchers have studied self-efficacy in various contexts (e.g., education, athletics, and business), and recently, self-efficacy has also started to draw attention from leadership researchers (Hannah et al., 2008; Kodama & Dugan, 2013; Machida & Schaubroeck, 2011; Ng, Ang, & Chan, 2008). Recently, Murphy and Johnson (2016) also discussed the roles of self-efficacy in students' leader development readiness. This chapter extends and offers an overview of the importance of self-efficacy in leadership effectiveness, a description of how self-efficacy could influence students' leadership competency development, and recommendations for developing leadership competencies through managing and fostering one's self-efficacy.

New Directions for Student Leadership, no. 156, Winter 2017 © 2017 Wiley Periodicals, Inc., A Wiley Company
Published online in Wiley Online Library (wileyonlinelibrary.com) • DOI: 10.1002/yd.20268

19

Defining Self-Efficacy in Leadership

In a larger framework of social cognitive theory (Bandura, 1997), which is also heavily studied in the context of education, self-efficacy has been identified as a construct that affects one's learning and achievement. Bandura (1997) posits that self-efficacy is central to human agency in any domain of life and further argues that positive self-efficacy beliefs influence one's achievement through their effects on one's emotions, cognitions, and actions. He asserts that when people are not efficacious about their abilities, they are less likely to challenge themselves and work toward their goals. Individuals with little self-efficacy beliefs are also more likely to fear the consequences of failing and discontinue their endeavor when they face adversities. On the other hand, when individuals have positive self-efficacy beliefs, they set challenging goals and show high degrees of commitment to achieving these goals. Such individuals also have a positive outlook in the face of obstacles and are resilient.

The roles of positive self-efficacy beliefs have been supported in research across various domains (Bandura, 1997). In studies on leadership, specifically, leader self-efficacy can be defined as leaders' perceived capabilities in areas needed to lead others effectively (Machida & Schaubroeck, 2011). One important tenet posed by Bandura (1997) is that self-efficacy is both task and context specific in each achievement area (e.g., individuals could have different degrees of self-efficacy beliefs for achieving tasks necessary for math versus English courses). Thus, in the context of leadership, self-efficacy should be specific to develop competencies for specific leadership tasks that are required at hand.

Several studies in management and business report the significant effects of leader self-efficacy on leadership effectiveness. For example, with a sample of managers in a real estate company, Paglis and Green (2002) demonstrated leader self-efficacy was positively related to leadership attempts toward changes. Hendricks and Payne (2007) further found that leader self-efficacy was related to subjective overall group performance in controlled experimental settings that had groups of four undergraduate students completing group tasks. Ng et al. (2008) also showed that leader self-efficacy played a mediating role in the relationship between personality and leader effectiveness among military leaders.

Compared with the studies on the relationship between leader self-efficacy and leadership effectiveness, research on the influences of leader self-efficacy on leadership competency development are scarce; however, the impacts can be inferred from the literature. For instance, with a sample of military cadets, Chemers, Watson, and May (2000) showed leader self-efficacy was positively related to leadership potential rated by their instructors. Chan and Drasgow (2001) demonstrated that military recruits' leader self-efficacy was positively related to motivation to lead and leadership potential rated by drill sergeants. Machida et al. (2016) also reported leader self-efficacy was related to leadership career ascendance among female college athletic administrators.

Relationship Between Self-Efficacy and the Development of Students' Leadership Competencies

Based on research regarding the roles of self-efficacy on leadership potential and career ascendance, self-efficacy is expected to have a positive impact on students' development of leadership competencies. However, before attempting to consider ways by which student self-efficacy can be nurtured, one needs to understand the potential effects of self-efficacy in one's competency development process; specifically, whether students should always maintain high leader self-efficacy, and whether leader self-efficacy is the only type of self-efficacy belief for students to develop as leaders.

Should Students Always Maintain High Leader Self-Efficacy?   In society, high degrees of confidence are generally considered desirable. And research discussed earlier in the chapter also point to high confidence or self-efficacy having positive impacts on leaders. However, thinking about the effects of leader self-efficacy on students' leadership, one should look at the context in which students are currently placed, specifically distinguishing whether students are in performance or preparatory contexts.

Bandura (1997) indicates the optimal level of self-efficacy may differ between when people are in situations where they are required to perform and achieve their task goals, that is in performance contexts, and when people are learning and preparing to achieve their performance, that is in preparatory contexts. Bandura argues that in performance contexts, self-efficacy should have positive and linear effects on performance. Thus, in the situations where students are required to perform certain leadership tasks (e.g., communicating the vision at a student organization meeting), the higher the self-efficacy students possess, the higher the performance they produce. The optimal level of self-efficacy in these contexts is a high level of self-efficacy. However, in preparatory contexts, where one is preparing and training to achieve a task goal and develop competencies (e.g., preparing the presentation of the vision to share at the student organization meeting), the effects of self-efficacy may not be linear. In fact, Bandura argues that moderately low self-efficacy may be the optimal level of self-efficacy for learning; both extremely low levels and extremely high levels of self-efficacy could hinder one's development of competencies.

Applying this concept of preparatory self-efficacy, Machida and Schaubroeck (2011) proposed that there is a curvilinear, inverted-U-shaped relationship between a magnitude of leader self-efficacy and one's learning of leadership competencies. Extremely low levels of leader self-efficacy may prevent students from taking on challenges, persisting in hardship, and committing to the development of their leadership skills. However, if students have extremely high levels of leader self-efficacy, or if they are too confident in their leadership abilities, they may become complacent and not put enough effort into developing their skills and competencies as leaders. Moderately low leader self-efficacy, or a little "self-doubt," could create healthy gaps between the current self and ideal self that would further facilitate their motivation to work hard toward development.

In the context of organizational learning and development, Lindsley, Brass, and Thomas (1995) posed that certain changes (increase or decrease) in either efficacy or performance should lead to similar changes in the other; for example, as one goes up, so does the other and vice versa. Accordingly, three patterns of efficacy changes are suggested. First is an upward spiral that involves more than three consecutive increases in efficacy and performance. Second is a downward spiral that involves more than three consecutive decreases in efficacy and performance. The last is the self-correcting cycle, which is a pattern where "a decrease in performance and efficacy is followed by an increase in performance or efficacy (or vice versa)" (Lindsley et al., 1995, p. 650).

Machida and Schaubroeck (2011) also suggest such a pattern is preferred for leaders' development. In upward spirals where students repeatedly increase leader self-efficacy and experience successes, students would not be able to engage in critical evaluations of their current state, and they would be less likely to put forth extra efforts and actively examine the new strategies that might further facilitate their learning of new leadership tasks. Downward spirals should also be avoided. In the quest for developing leadership competencies, students may face many failures that could make them believe that they have little potential to develop as leaders, which could lead them to experience a state of learned helplessness (Machida & Schaubroeck, 2011). It is important that students avoid being stuck in debilitating upward or downward spirals but instead aim to stay in the self-correcting cycle for optimal leader self-efficacy changes.

Not much support is yet available for the benefits of a moderate level of preparatory leader self-efficacy or benefits of self-correcting cycles of leader self-efficacy changes, but scholars in other contexts also propose a similar effect (Feltz & Wood, 2009). This is an area of research that needs further pursuit. But for now, to respond to the question "Should students always maintain high leader self-efficacy?" the theory and research would support the notion that students should generally maintain moderately low leader self-efficacy, but students should stay in a self-correcting cycle of leader self-efficacy changes, where lowered leader self-efficacy or performance is followed by an increase in leader self-efficacy or performance.

Is Leader Self-Efficacy the Only Relevant Self-Efficacy Belief for Students to Develop as Leaders?   Leader self-efficacy should have a significant influence on students' leadership competency development. However, as discussed, self-efficacy is a domain-dependent construct that is specific to the task at hand (Bandura, 1997). Are there other types of self-efficacy that are relevant to students' development of leadership knowledge and competencies? In addition to considering the influences of leader self-efficacy, one needs to examine the impact of learning self-efficacy. Learning self-efficacy can be defined as beliefs regarding one's capability for learning new skills and utilizing the learned skills in performance situations (Pintrich, Smith, Garcia, & McKeachie, 1991; Reichard & Thompson, 2016). This type of self-efficacy can be distinguished from leader self-efficacy, a belief regarding one's abilities to perform leadership tasks. Learning self-efficacy in the context of leadership competency development involves believing one has the capabilities to learn leadership skills to achieve the leadership task, and can also be described as leader developmental efficacy, defined as the "beliefs about her ability to change and develop her current leadership skills" (Murphy & Johnson, 2016, p. 73) and has been considered to influence students' efforts toward their leader development.

In his original work, Bandura (1997) also asserts that learning self-efficacy is critical for one's development. It allows people to engage in adaptive thoughts and behavioral processes that facilitate their persistence (Bandura & Locke, 2003). Without such a belief, it would be difficult to maintain a high motivation to learn (Bandura, 1997). Thus, there would be a positive linear relationship between learning self-efficacy and students' development of leadership competencies. Though little research has been done regarding the relationship between learning self-efficacy and leadership competency development, research in education consistently demonstrates the importance of learning self-efficacy in students' learning and skill acquisition (Lodewyk & Winne, 2005), and scholars in leadership research suggest its positive relationship (Hannah et al., 2008; Machida & Schaubroeck, 2011).

Further, students need learning self-efficacy that is resilient when developing their leadership competencies. Self-efficacy is conceptualized to be a fluctuating property that is prone to change depending on the situation (Bandura, 1997). Thus, self-efficacy could be fragile and easily affected by various factors. Bandura argues for the importance of resilient self-efficacy that is "firmly established" (p. 68), especially for overcoming the obstacles and roadblocks in one's endeavor. Individuals who have fragile self-efficacy beliefs can be easily discouraged to further their efforts in the face of adversities. Resilient self-efficacy can allow individuals to persevere through these adversities.

Thus, there may be a great benefit to fluctuations in leader self-efficacy; that is self-correcting cycles of leader self-efficacy changes for the optimal development of students' leadership competencies. However, students may face many failures in their process of developing as leaders that could lead to lowered leader self-efficacy and debilitating downward spirals. Resilient learning self-efficacy that is resistant to change would prevent students from experiencing such devastating cycles of failures and decreases in leader self-efficacy. To respond to the question, "Is leader self-efficacy the only relevant self-efficacy belief for students to develop as leaders?" the theory and

Table 2.1   Influence of Various Types of Self-Efficacy on Leader
Development

Type of self-efficacy	Context	Desired level of self-efficacy	Desired changes in self-efficacy
Leader self-efficacy	Preparatory	Moderately low level	Self-correcting cycles (lowered self-efficacy followed by an increase in self-efficacy)
	Performance	High level	High and resilient (high self-efficacy maintained throughout)
Learning self-efficacy	Both in preparatory and performance context	High level	High and resilient (high self-efficacy maintained throughout)

research would support the idea that students should maintain resilient learning self-efficacy for the optimal development of their leadership competencies. Table 2.1 provides a summary of the influence of various types of self-efficacy on leader development.

Nurturing and Managing Leader Self-Efficacy of Students

In order to apply these concepts to developing students' leadership competencies, it is critical to understand the sources of students' self-efficacy. Social cognitive theory posits there are four main sources of self-efficacy (Bandura, 1997). The first is enactive mastery experiences, which include past experiences of successes in the particular task and are considered the strongest sources of self-efficacy. Second are vicarious experiences, which encompass the modeling or observing of the others' competence and achievement. Third is verbal persuasion, which is related to others' appraisal and demonstration of support for one's ability to succeed (Bandura, 1997). The fourth is affective and physiological states, which involve how changes in emotions and physiological reactions may be associated with changes in self-efficacy. Based on these four sources of self-efficacy and theory and research on leadership, the following outlines personal and environmental factors that may affect students' self-efficacy and recommendations for leadership development practices.

Considering Students' Personal Factors. The following section identifies two personal factors that need to be considered in developing leadership competencies of students: learning orientation and gender.

NEW DIRECTIONS FOR STUDENT LEADERSHIP • DOI: 10.1002/yd

Learning Orientation. Scholars (DeRue & Wellman, 2009; Dragoni et al., 2009; Van Velsor et al., 2010) have argued there is variation in the degrees of learning that occurs from similar developmental experiences, and such variation can be attributed to individual differences in the ability to learn. Learning orientation (Dweck, 1975) may reflect such ability. Learning orientation is a psychological construct that has been discussed heavily in an educational context and among leader development researchers (DeRue & Wellman, 2009; Dragoni et al., 2009). Although performance orientation focuses on comparison with others toward gaining a favorable outcome, learning orientation can be defined as an emphasis on learning, mastery, and increasing competence (Dweck, 1975). Though students with high-performance orientations seek to engage in immediate performance, students with high learning orientation are motivated to investigate new methods and tactics, which may improve one's capabilities for the longer term (Dweck, 1975). Research indicates learning orientation is associated with individuals' willingness to participate and engage in developmental experiences, which in turn influences their own development (DeRue & Wellman, 2009; Dragoni et al., 2009).

As scholars (Lindsley et al., 1995; Machida & Schaubroeck, 2011) suggest, learning orientation should be directly related to students' leader self-efficacy. Instead of focusing on comparison with others and getting immediate outcomes, focusing on acquisition and development of skills should help them maintain moderately low levels of leader self-efficacy and maintenance of the self-correcting cycles. Students with high learning orientation would critically examine their progress in their leadership competency development. Thus, they would be less likely to experience upward efficacy spirals. They would also focus on their own individual learning and not on gaining favorable outcomes; thus, they would not be easily discouraged when they received unfavorable results and evaluations from others and would not be stuck in downward efficacy spirals.

As Bandura (1997) indicates, successes or mastery experiences are the strongest sources of self-efficacy. Accumulating successes that are defined by learning should lead to an increase in self-efficacy regarding the ability to learn. In the college environment where students are constantly evaluated and compared, it is easy for them to discredit learning and adopt a performance orientation. On a regular basis, they compete for high GPAs, securing one of only a few internship positions, getting into graduate school, and so on; the current college environment could be supporting the notion of performance rather than learning. Thus, for faculty, academic advisors, staff, or parents that are concerned about students' leadership competency development, it is recommended they make a conscious effort to focus on and reward students' efforts around learning instead of tangible outcomes (performance), which would foster their growth mindset that they can change their abilities, and in turn assist in their adoption of learning orientation (Dweck, 1986).

Influences of Gender.   Though women are equally qualified as leaders and some studies even suggest women may have better leadership skills (Eagly & Chin, 2010), scholars indicate they may hesitate to take on leadership roles because of low self-efficacy beliefs about themselves as leaders (Betz, 2007; Hacket & Betz, 1981). Such differences may create a discrepancy in their career attainment; studies have consistently reported women show low self-efficacy and low ambitions to advance their leadership careers (Machida, Schaubroeck, Ewing, Gould, & Feltz, 2016; Stewart & Shapiro, 2000; van Vianen & Keizer, 1996). Betz (2007) and Hacket and Betz (1981) argue that low self-efficacy beliefs of women may be the result of limited access to positive self-efficacy information sources (i.e., enactive mastery experiences, verbal persuasion, vicarious experiences, and affective and physiological states) proposed by Bandura (1997). Though scarce, existing research does support this claim. van Vianen and Keizer (1996) showed that men reported higher degrees of managerial experiences and job tasks than women and received more positive feedback or verbal persuasion for their work, resulting in men having higher managerial self-efficacy and higher ambitions for managerial careers as compared with women. Machida et al. (2016) also showed that women are less exposed to challenges as compared with men in athletic coaching fields and women showed lower leader self-efficacy and intentions to advance their coaching leadership careers. Women also generally report higher ratings of family–work conflict (Ernst-Kossek & Ozeki, 1998; Hoobler, Wayne, & Lemmon, 2009); research indicates this could pose significant stress and negative emotions that could lower their self-efficacy (Machida et al., 2016).

When developing leadership competencies of students, one needs to consider gender differences in self-efficacy that may exist. Some women may not seem as motivated to engage in and seek out experiences that assist them in developing their competencies as leaders. This apparent lack of motivation may actually be due to their low self-efficacy beliefs as leaders and limited experiences of exposure to positive sources of leader self-efficacy. Thus, some female students may need extra resources and support to help them foster their leader self-efficacy.

Considering Environments Surrounding Students.   A college environment that provides students with quality developmental experiences is necessary for nurturing and managing students' self-efficacy for leadership competency development. McCauley, DeRue, Yost, and Taylor (2013) argue that the developmental experiences that have an influential effect on students' self-efficacy in leadership consist of three main components: challenges, feedback, and support.

Challenges.   Challenges help students push their boundaries and expand their comfort zones (Van Velsor et al., 2010). A comfortable environment limits students' opportunity for growth. Such environments discourage students from seeking new knowledge or skills and motivate them to grow. Challenges, reframed as "opportunities," however, allow them to cultivate their adaptive perspectives (Van Velsor et al., 2010).

Empirical research supports the effects of challenges on leader development (DeRue & Wellman, 2009; Dragoni et al., 2009), and some recent studies reported that challenges are related to leader self-efficacy (Machida et al., 2016). Challenges can tap into the strongest sources of self-efficacy described by Bandura (1997), enactive mastery experiences. Challenges provide students with opportunities to fail, which may lower their self-efficacy to the optimal level and prevent them from inflating their sense of self-efficacy. By installing self-doubts, they can seek out resources and new ways in which they can overcome challenges. When they overcome challenges, they gain the successful learning experience, which should increase positive efficacy beliefs not only regarding their leadership competencies (which can lead them into a self-correcting cycle) but also regarding their ability to learn. McCauley et al. (2013) identified 10 challenges that can help students develop as leaders. These include dealing with unfamiliar responsibilities, taking on new directions, confronting inherited problems, dealing with problems with employees, engaging in work that is high stakes, expanding one's scope and scale, facing external pressure, influencing others without authority, working across cultures, and embracing workgroup diversity.

Feedback.   Performance evaluations or feedback that students obtain from themselves, teachers, peers, and family can also be critical (Van Velsor et al., 2010) to enhancing self-efficacy. Getting feedback allows students to examine their current state and identify areas for development. (Van Velsor et al., 2010).

Feedback is related to another important source of self-efficacy, verbal persuasion. Students can increase their efficacy belief by the verbal encouragement from others and decrease it when they gain critical feedback. Thus, feedback can provide students with "realistic" information regarding their abilities as leaders. When they are in downward efficacy spirals, positive and instructive feedback can help them to clarify the ways by which they could deal with the setbacks in their leadership activities. When they are in upward efficacy spirals, critical feedback about their current state can lower their leader self-efficacy to the appropriate level and work harder for their leadership goals.

Support.   The third component of self-efficacy is support from others (Van Velsor et al., 2010). Through facing challenges, students will be provided with opportunities for further growth; however, they may feel insecurity in these experiences. Providing support that confirms that their learning during these challenges can lessen this sense of insecurity, help them deal with struggles, and maintain adaptive views of themselves (Van Velsor et al., 2010).

Similar to feedback, support is related to verbal persuasion sources of self-efficacy and can provide students with the information that helps maintain self-efficacy beliefs in highly challenging situations, thus preventing them from experiencing downward efficacy spirals. Support is also related to physiological and affective states. As Bandura (1997) indicates, strategies to decrease stress and increase positive emotions are important ways to increase one's adaptive self-efficacy beliefs. Continuous support from others has a significant impact on students' self-efficacy. Provision of these experiences can be formal (e.g., through semester-long leader development workshops and programs) or informal (e.g., through department advising sessions), but it is recommended to invest conscious efforts in providing students with support to nurture and manage their self-efficacy in their leadership competency development.

One important form of support that demands special attention is mentoring. The benefits of mentoring, role modeling, and other developmental relationships in one's career development are well documented and supported (Allen et al., 2004; Day, 2001). McCauley and colleagues (2013) also argued that quality mentoring relationships provide both career-enhancing effects and psychological support to leaders, whether it is formal, as a mentor assigned to a mentee, or informal, as encouraged by the organization (Day, 2001). Regardless of the formality of the mentoring relationship, scholars argue mentoring relationships can offer a powerful developmental experience providing support to developing leaders (Day, 2001). Mentoring relationships also provide leaders with opportunities to observe and interact with senior leaders, which can assist developing leaders to refine their strategic thinking critical for advancing their careers (Day, 2001). In addition to providing verbal persuasion as a form of support, mentoring can also provide students with the opportunity for vicarious experiences or to observe and model the leadership behaviors, which is also one of the main sources of self-efficacy identified by Bandura (1997). Thus, whether formal or informal with faculty advisors or senior students, students may be provided with mentors who can model the appropriate leader competency and self-efficacy themselves. Such modeling can be a powerful source of self-efficacy for students engaging in leadership competency development.

Conclusion

Student leadership competency development is a complicated phenomenon and cannot be easily accomplished. However, the degrees of strength in beliefs that one can lead successfully and that one can learn to be a leader make a significant difference in students' leadership competency development. In conjunction with the various factors that are introduced in this issue regarding leadership competency development, self-efficacy concepts can assist students in their endeavor to develop as better leaders.

References

Allen, T. D., Eby, L. T., Poteet, M. L., & Lentz, E. (2004). Career benefits associated with mentoring for protégés: A meta-analysis. *Journal of Applied Psychology, 89,* 127–136.

Bandura, A. (1997). *Self-efficacy: The exercise of control.* New York, NY: W.H. Freeman.

Bandura, A., & Locke, E. A. (2003). Negative self-efficacy effects revisited. *Journal of Applied Psychology, 88,* 87–89.

Betz, N. E. (2007). Career self-efficacy: Exemplary recent research and emerging directions. *Journal of Career Assessment, 15,* 403–422.

Chan, K. Y., & Drasgow, F. (2001). Toward a theory of individual differences and leadership: Understanding the motivation to lead. *Journal of Applied Psychology, 86,* 481–498.

Chemers, M. M., Watson, C. B., & May, S. T. (2000). Dispositional affect and leadership effectiveness: A comparison of self-esteem, optimism, and efficacy. *Personality and Social Psychology Bulletin, 26,* 267–277.

Day, D. V. (2001). Leadership development: A review in context. *Leadership Quarterly, 11,* 581–613.

DeRue, S. D., & Wellman, N. (2009). Developing leaders via experience: The role of developmental challenge, learning orientation, and feedback availability. *Journal of Applied Psychology, 94,* 859–875.

Dragoni, L., Tesluk, P. E., Russell, J. E. A., & Oh, I. S. (2009). Understanding managerial development: Integrating developmental assignments, learning orientation, and access to developmental opportunities in predicting managerial competencies. *Academy of Management Journal, 52,* 731–743.

Dweck, C. S. (1975). The role of expectations and attributions in the alleviation of learned helplessness. *Journal of Personality and Social Psychology, 31,* 674–685.

Dweck, C. S. (1986). Motivational processes affecting learning. *American Psychologist, 41,* 1040–1048.

Eagly, A. H., & Chin, J. L. (2010). Diversity in leadership in a changing world. *American Psychologist, 65,* 216–224.

Ernst-Kossek, E., & Ozeki, C. (1998). Work–family conflict, policies, and the job–life satisfaction relationship: A review and directions for organizational behavior–human resources research. *Journal of Applied Psychology, 83,* 139.

Feltz, D. L., & Wood, M. (2009). Can self-doubt be beneficial to performance? Exploring the concept of preparatory efficacy. *The Open Sports Sciences Journal, 2,* 65–70.

Hacket, G., & Betz, N. E. (1981). A self-efficacy approach to the career development of women. *Journal of Vocational Behavior, 18,* 326–339.

Hannah, S. T., Avolio, B. J., Luthans, F., & Harms, P. D. (2008). Leadership efficacy: Review and future directions. *The Leadership Quarterly, 19,* 669–692.

Hendricks, J., & Payne, S. (2007). Beyond the big five: Leader goal orientation as a predictor of leadership effectiveness. *Human Performance, 20,* 317–343.

Hoobler, J. M., Wayne, S. J., & Lemmon, G. (2009). Bosses' perceptions of family-work conflict and women's promotability: Glass ceiling effects. *Academy of Management Journal, 52,* 939–957.

Kodama, C., & Dugan, J. P. (2013). Leveraging leadership efficacy in college students: Disaggregating data to examine unique predictors by race. *Equity & Excellence in Education, 46,* 184–201.

Lindsley, D. H., Brass, D. J., & Thomas, J. B. (1995). Efficacy–performance spirals: A multilevel perspective. *Academy of Management Review, 20,* 645–678.

Lodewyk, K. R., & Winne, P. H. (2005). Relations among the structure of learning tasks, achievement, and changes in self-efficacy in secondary students. *Journal of Educational Psychology, 97,* 3–12. https://doi.org/10.1037/0022-0663.97.1.3

Machida, M., & Schaubroeck, J. (2011). The role of self-efficacy beliefs in leader development. *Journal of Leadership and Organizational Studies, 18,* 459–468.

Machida, M., Schaubroeck, J., Gould, D., Ewing, M., & Feltz, D. L. (2016). What influences collegiate coaches' intentions to advance their leadership careers? The roles of leader self-efficacy and outcome expectancies. *International Sport Coaching Journal*.

Machida-Kosuga, M., Schaubroeck, J., & Feltz, D. L. (2016). Leader self-efficacy of women intercollegiate athletic administrators: A look at barriers and developmental antecedents. *Journal of Intercollegiate Sport, 9*, 157–178.

McCauley, C. D., DeRue, D. S., Yost, P. R., & Taylor, S. (2013). *Experience-driven leader development: Models, tools, best practices, and advice for on-the-job development.* Hoboken, NJ: John Wiley & Sons.

Murphy, S. E., & Johnson, S. K. (2016). Leadership and leader developmental self-efficacy: Their role in enhancing leader development efforts. *New Directions for Student Leadership, 149*, 73–84.

Ng, K. Y., Ang, S., & Chan, K. Y. (2008). Personality and leader effectiveness: A moderated mediation model of leadership self-efficacy, job demands, and job autonomy. *Journal of Applied Psychology, 93*, 733–743.

Paglis, L. L., & Green, S. G. (2002). Leadership self-efficacy and managers' motivation for leading change. *Journal of Organizational Behavior, 23*, 215–235.

Pintrich, P. R., Smith, D. A., Garcia, T., & McKeachie, W. J. (1991). *A manual for the use of the motivated strategies for learning questionnaire (MSLQ)* (Technical Report No. 91-b-004). Ann Arbor, MI: University of Michigan, School of Education.

Reichard, R., & Thompson, S. (Eds.). (2016). *New Directions for Student Leadership, 149.*

Stewart, M. M., & Shapiro, D. L. (2000). Selection based on merit versus demography: Implications across race and gender lines. *Journal of Applied Psychology, 85*, 219–231.

Van Velsor, E., McCauley, C. D., & Ruderman, M. N. (2010). *The Center for Creative Leadership handbook of leadership development.* San Francisco, CA: Jossey-Bass.

van Vianen, A. E. M., & Keizer, W. A. J. (1996). Gender differences in managerial intention. *Gender, Work, and Organization, 3*, 103–114.

Moe Machida-Kosuga is an assistant professor in the School of Physical Education at Osaka University of Health and Sport Sciences, Japan.

New Directions for Student Leadership • DOI: 10.1002/yd

This chapter describes how to use a leadership competency approach to help students develop their five signature themes from the Clifton StrengthsFinder assessment into strengths.

Using Leadership Competencies to Develop Talents into Strengths

Corey Seemiller

Strengths-based education is widely used in colleges and universities today (Gallup, Inc., 2015a) and involves helping students leverage their natural talents instead of trying to focus on remediating weaknesses (Passarelli, Hall, & Anderson, 2010). With its roots in positive psychology, "the scientific study of optimal human functioning" (Sheldon, Frederickson, Rathunde, & Csikszentmihalyi, 2000, para. 2), helping students tap into their strengths can promote success and achievement in college (Louis, 2011).

Several instruments are available to help students identify their talents and strengths. These include the Clifton StrengthsFinder (Rath, 2007), the VIA Survey (Peterson & Seligman, 2004), the R2 Strengths Profiler (Centre for Applied Positive Psychology, 2009), and the Strengths Portrait[1] (Total SDI, n.d.). The Clifton StrengthsFinder, in particular, is part of Gallup, Inc.'s StrengthsQuest program, which is used by more than 600 schools and colleges (Gallup, Inc., 2015a). StrengthsQuest is integrated into first-year programs, academic courses, co-curricular involvement experiences, and leadership programs within higher education (Louis, 2012). Its use is so prominent in leadership programs that the third edition of Exploring Leadership (Komives, Lucas, & McMahon, 2013) includes an individual code for students to take the Clifton StrengthsFinder. Because of its widespread use in higher education (Lopez & Louis, 2009) and prominence in leadership development, the Clifton StrengthsFinder will serve as the context for the approach to competency development described in this chapter. This chapter will offer an overview of the Clifton StrengthsFinder including the difference between talent identification and strengths development, a description of how to use competencies to develop talents into strengths, a process for mapping competencies and strengths, and steps for using competencies and strengths together.

NEW DIRECTIONS FOR STUDENT LEADERSHIP, no. 156, Winter 2017 © 2017 Wiley Periodicals, Inc., A Wiley Company
Published online in Wiley Online Library (wileyonlinelibrary.com) • DOI: 10.1002/yd.20269

Clifton StrengthsFinder

In 1998, Don Clifton and a team of experts created an assessment to measure one's innate strengths, which are "talents that have been developed to produce consistent levels of excellent performance in a particular activity" (Clifton & Anderson, 2002 in Louis, 2012, p. 2). Clifton believed there were benefits both personally and organizationally for people to focus on what they do well instead of attempting to enhance weaknesses (Clifton & Harter, 2003). Based on Clifton's work, the Gallup, Inc. organization has spent more than a decade in designing and offering strengths-based programs that include assessments, training sessions, curriculum, research, and even courses designed to help individuals understand, develop, and apply their strengths and the strengths of others.

The Clifton StrengthsFinder[2] is an online assessment that measures one's talent themes, or what Hodges and Clifton (2004) refer to as "naturally recurring patterns of thought, feeling, or behavior that can be productively applied" (p. 257). With 34 talent themes, results from the instrument showcase only an individual's top five signature themes, allowing the focus to be on what one does well and not what theme might be listed in the 34th spot on the list. Because of the name of the assessment, it might appear that the results showcase one's top five strengths. However, the results provide a list of the top five talent themes that, when developed, have the greatest potential for becoming strengths (Buckingham & Clifton, 2001).

With a test–retest reliability estimate of 0.70 across the 34 themes, the instrument meets the accepted instrument stability standards of the American Educational Research Association, American Psychological Association, and National Council on Measurement in Education (Schreiner, 2006). The Clifton StrengthsFinder is grounded in more than 30 years of research across a variety of sectors in more than 30 countries (Hodges & Clifton, 2004).

Many studies have been conducted related to strengths in higher education. Passarelli et al. (2010) found that using a strengths approach in outdoor education resulted in students reporting greater levels of personal growth and enhancing their personal relationships. Understanding one's personal strengths is also related to higher GPAs (Hodges & Clifton, 2004), as well as increased personal confidence and greater gains in effective leadership practices (Louis, 2011).

Talent Identification.   Many strengths-based programs involve helping students become aware of their talents (Louis, 2012). In many cases, students take the Clifton StrengthsFinder and receive a list of their top five signature themes. Talent identification can be beneficial regarding self-efficacy, academic motivation, academic control, personal growth, and academic engagement, among others (Louis, 2012). But Buckingham (2007) asserts "when it comes to the strengths movement, we are stuck in the first stage. We know how to label. We don't know how to move beyond a label and actually put our strengths to work" (p. 11). This is apparent in that many strengths development programs on campuses are actually Clifton StrengthsFinder interpretations designed to solely help students understand their results (Louis, 2011). And these results can be misrepresented as "strengths" and not more accurately as "talent themes."

Strengths Development. Although there are benefits related to talent identification, even literature put out by Gallup, Inc. (2015b) emphasizes utilizing strengths is more than just creating awareness. It is about developing talents into strengths (Gallup, Inc.,2015b), like a natural athlete or musician learning techniques to best master their craft.

The misnomer that one's results on the assessment are strengths and not actually talent themes supports a fixed mind-set (Dweck, 1999), one in which "trait-like qualities" are not easily responsive to developmental efforts (Louis, 2011). This says to individuals, "You are great at these five things. There is nothing more you need to or can do to accentuate them. Just live from your strengths." However, approaching strengths from the perspective of a growth mind-set (Dweck, 1999), one that purports trait-like qualities can be responsive to developmental efforts, better aligns with the true philosophy of strengths. Although talents may not change significantly over time, these talents can be developed into strengths (Hodges & Clifton, 2004). Louis (2008) found that students who experienced a developmental approach to strengths rather than solely talent identification veered more toward a growth mind-set rather than a fixed mind-set.

Few studies, though, have been done that describe how students can intentionally develop their top five talent themes into strengths. Bowers and Lopez (2010) found to best capitalize on strengths, students need continual social support, experiences of success, and reinforcement of personal strengths. In addition, simply increasing one's frequency of use can polish talents into strengths (Buckingham & Clifton, 2001). For example, Lopez and Louis (2009) assert that students need to participate in meaningful opportunities and experiences in which they can utilize their strengths to truly develop them. Both studies highlight application as a way to develop talents into strengths.

In addition to developing strengths through experience, strengths can also be developed by enhancing appropriate knowledge and skills (Clifton & Anderson, 2002; Hodges & Clifton, 2004). There is little information that identifies what knowledge and skills are connected to strengths development as well as a process for using this approach. One method that may provide the link between knowledge/skills enhancement and strengths development is a competency approach.

Competencies

Competencies are defined as "the collection of knowledge, skills and attitudes" (Mulder, Gulikers, Wesselink, & Biemans, 2008, p. 8) that contribute to one's effectiveness in completing a task or role (Seemiller, 2013). Some competency researchers believe being effective is being able to do a job at the minimal required level resulting in adequate performance, whereas others believe being effective is being able to excel at a job resulting in "star" performance (Robbins, Bradley, & Spicer, 2001). Considering the context of higher education is an environment for learning, it is critical to focus on baseline development of essential competencies rather than foster a "star" mentality.

Using Competencies.   As noted in Chapter 1, competencies are utilized across sectors and are prevalent in educational settings, businesses, and professional associations (Conger & Ready, 2004). They are used in an "attempt to leverage the experience, lessons learned, and knowledge of seasoned leaders for the benefit of others and the organization" (Hollenbeck, McCall, & Silzer, 2006, p. 403). Referred to as the "North Star," competencies can be used to navigate what the organization desires in order to create better outcomes (Intagliata, Ulrich, & Smallwood, 2000, p. 3).

By identifying critical competencies, organizations can define what success looks like, and members can learn and develop the competencies they need to be successful (Intagliata et al., 2000). This allows organizations the ability to operationalize their training to focus on the development of particular competencies (Ennis, 2008; Wright et al., 2000). In addition, competency development and proficiency are measurable (Wright et al., 2000), creating an ability to evaluate employees with set criteria (Posthuma & Campion, 2008). Evaluations are often in the form of 360-degree feedback to help clarify one's growth and performance in particular competencies (Tornow, London, & CCL Associates, 1998, in Intagliata et al., 2000).

In a higher education setting, specifically, competencies can be integrated into lesson plans in credit-bearing courses or co-curricular experiences to provide a learning framework as well as create a means for the educator to assess learning and development of those competencies (Seemiller, 2013). With the call to move beyond talent identification and toward strengths development (Buckingham, 2007; Louis, 2008), a competency approach could provide a useful roadmap for helping students develop talents into strengths. By developing a particular competency associated with a talent theme, one might be able to better leverage that talent into a strength (see Figure 3.1).

For example, by developing the competency of Problem Solving, an individual could be more skilled at figuring out the underlying cause of a

Figure 3.1.   Strengths Development

Talent Identification + Competency Enhancement = Strengths Development

NEW DIRECTIONS FOR STUDENT LEADERSHIP • DOI: 10.1002/yd

problem, identifying potential solutions, and selecting the most appropriate solution. Developing this competency could contribute to the development of the Restorative strength from the Clifton StrengthsFinder because this strength is about making improvements to processes, items, or even people. Being able to discover the underlying cause of why something needs improvement might help that person approach the restoration process in a more informed manner.

Mapping Competencies and Strengths

To enhance one's competencies and thus develop one's strengths, it is essential to know which competencies are related to which talent themes from Gallup, Inc. Given the robust methodology and the comprehensive nature of the study, the Student Leadership Competencies were selected as the list of competencies to match with talent themes. The Student Leadership Competencies were derived from an analysis of learning outcomes from all 522 accredited academic programs in the United States (Seemiller, 2013). The 60 competencies are clustered in eight conceptual categories: Learning and Reasoning, Self-Awareness and Development, Group Dynamics, Interpersonal Interaction, Civic Responsibility, Communication, Strategic Planning, and Personal Behavior.

The matching process involved using content analysis of the established text definitions of the 34 talent themes listed on the Quick Reference Card from Gallup, Inc. (2012) and the definitions of the 60 Student Leadership Competencies from the Student Leadership Competencies Guidebook (Seemiller, 2013). Because the content for both the talent themes and competencies were already available, no additional data collection was necessary. The content analysis process involved a deductive approach in cross-comparing both theories for similar phenomena (Elo & Kyngas, 2007). Definitions for each talent theme and competency were coded for similarities between each (synonymous concepts) as well as cause-and-effect relationships (e.g., to possess [talent theme], one would need to effectively do [competency]). Because the focus of this chapter is to enhance strengths development, the analysis involved looking specifically at the competencies related to each strength and not the other way around.

Through this process, the broad nature of talent themes yielded many associated competencies. Each talent theme was associated with a minimum of 3 leadership competencies and a maximum of 10. Thirty of the 34 talent themes were comprised of competencies from more than one category from the Student Leadership Competencies, highlighting the breadth of most talent themes. Table 3.1 lists the competencies associated with each talent theme.

New Directions for Student Leadership • DOI: 10.1002/yd

Table 3.1   Associated Competencies for Each Talent Theme

Talent Themes (Gallup, Inc.)	Associated Student Leadership Competencies (Seemiller, 2013)
Achiever®	Initiative, Follow-Through, Resiliency, Plan, Excellence
Activator®	Decision-Making, Initiative, Follow-Through, Creating Change
Adaptability®	Other Perspectives, Responding to Ambiguity, Responding to Change, Resiliency, Positive Attitude
Analytical®	Reflection and Application, Systems Thinking, Analysis, Organizational Behavior
Arranger™	Synthesis, Evaluation, Problem Solving, Responding to Ambiguity, Plan, Organization, Others' Contributions
Belief®	Self-Understanding, Personal Values, Ethics
Command®	Decision-Making, Initiative, Functioning Independently, Confidence, Verbal Communication, Advocating for a Point of View, Motivation, Appropriate Interaction
Communication®	Verbal Communication, Nonverbal Communication, Listening, Facilitation, Writing
Competition®	Personal Contributions, Confidence, Excellence, Goals
Connectedness®	Personal Values, Confidence, Responsibility for Personal Behavior
Consistency®	Ethics, Social Responsibility, Plan
Context®	Research, Reflection and Application, Systems Thinking, Analysis, Others' Circumstances
Deliberative®	Research, Other Perspectives, Reflection and Application, Analysis, Evaluation, Decision-Making, Plan
Developer®	Others' Circumstances, Appropriate Interaction, Empathy, Mentoring Motivation, Others' Contributions, Empowerment, Providing Feedback
Discipline™	Functioning Independently, Follow-Through, Excellence, Goals, Plan, Organization
Empathy™	Other Perspectives, Others' Circumstances, Listening, Appropriate Interaction, Empathy
Focus™	Evaluation, Initiative, Follow-Through, Resiliency, Organization
Futuristic®	Reflection and Application, Idea Generation, Vision
Harmony®	Group Development, Appropriate Interaction, Listening, Facilitation, Conflict Negotiation, Others' Contributions, Positive Attitude
Ideation®	Other Perspectives, Systems Thinking, Idea Generation, Problem Solving, Vision
Includer®	Diversity, Others' Circumstances, Inclusion, Appropriate Interaction, Empathy, Collaboration
Individualization®	Diversity, Others' Circumstances, Other Perspectives, Others' Contributions
Input®	Research, Other Perspectives, Synthesis, Idea Generation

(Continued)

NEW DIRECTIONS FOR STUDENT LEADERSHIP • DOI: 10.1002/yd

Table 3.1   Continued

Talent Themes (Gallup, Inc.)	Associated Student Leadership Competencies (Seemiller, 2013)
Intellection®	Research, Other Perspectives, Reflection and Application, Systems Thinking, Analysis, Idea Generation, Problem Solving
Learner®	Research, Other Perspectives, Idea Generation, Others' Circumstances, Self-Development
Maximizer®	Other Perspectives, Reflection and Application, Scope of Competence, Excellence, Vision
Positivity®	Positive Attitude, Resiliency, Motivation
Relator®	Productive Relationships, Appropriate Interaction, Mentoring, Supervision, Collaboration
Responsibility®	Helping Others, Service, Follow-Through, Responsibility for Personal Behavior, Ethics, Resiliency, Excellence
Restorative®	Reflection and Application, Problem Solving, Excellence
Self-Assurance®	Personal Values, Ethics, Confidence
Significance®	Functioning Independently, Responsibility for Personal Behavior, Ethics, Excellence, Receiving Feedback, Personal Contributions
Strategic™	Systems Thinking, Analysis, Idea Generation, Problem Solving, Decision-Making, Power Dynamics, Mission, Vision, Goals, Plan
Woo®	Verbal Communication, Nonverbal Communication, Listening, Advocating for a Point of View, Appropriate Interaction, Motivation

Using Competencies and Strengths Together

Being able to narrow down from a much larger list of competencies to only those associated with one's talent themes can serve as a roadmap for students in their leadership development. The following are recommended steps for helping students utilize competencies to develop their talent themes into strengths.

Step 1: Identify Talent Themes.   Have students identify their top five talent themes by taking the Clifton StrengthsFinder. During this step, it is important that students have an awareness of their talent themes so that they can best develop them later. Strategies for increasing awareness include interpretation workshops, one-on-one advising, or having students read books/articles on strengths. Because many campuses already integrate Gallup's StrengthsQuest program into orientation, courses, programs, and workshops, this step might already be instituted.

Step 2: Create a Personal Competency List.   Have students list all the competencies (from Table 3.1) associated with their top five talent themes to create their personal competency list. If a competency is associated with more than one of their themes, they only need to list it once. This is critical so that students can narrow their focus to only those competencies related to their talent themes. During this step, students should learn about the competencies on their list, reflecting on why they are important and how enhancing each of the competencies can help them leverage their talents into strengths. Students can learn this through content presented in a workshop or course, or through their own research and reflection.

Step 3: Assess Competency Proficiency.   Have students assess their proficiency for the competencies on their personal competency list. One method to do this includes having the students take self-assessments. They can take an inventory related to a particular competency or cluster of competencies (like one focused only on problem-solving or communication) or complete a holistic assessment, such as the Student Leadership Competencies Inventory (Seemiller, 2016), which specifically measures all 60 competencies. Another method for assessing their skill level is to solicit external feedback. Students can use a 360 evaluation in which external observers assess the student's competency levels on a preset scale. There are many 360 evaluation tools available to use or adapt for this purpose as well as observer rubrics that can provide useful feedback. In addition, students can receive external feedback through discussions with a supervisor, advisor, coach, and/or mentor to uncover any competencies that need enhancement.

Step 4: Set Competency Enhancement Goals.   Using findings from the self-assessments and/or external feedback, have students identify the competencies from their personal competency list they would like to enhance. Once they have selected one or more competencies, they should develop specific goals and plans. For example, a student may want to focus on Verbal Communication specifically around public speaking. That student's goal might involve taking a speech class and earning an A. Another student might focus on Verbal Communication as well and set the goal of attending three seminars on public speaking and then give a speech that external observers evaluate for the effective use of the competency of Verbal Communication.

Step 5: Engage in Competency Enhancement Experiences.   Have students participate in training, workshops, courses, experiences, and/or programs to that align with their goals. Some students may set a goal in which they do not know the resources, programs, or experiences available to achieve that goal. So, it is important to find ways to connect students to competency-enhancing experiences.

Step 6: Assess Competency Enhancement and Strengths Development.   After the student completes any competency enhancement goals, have the student again assess their skill levels in those competencies.

Students can use the same instruments or processes used when they first engaged in competency assessment. In addition, it is important to see to what extent enhancing a competency leads to strengths development. Providing an opportunity for self-reflection as well as external feedback can help students make meaning of the development of their strengths.

Benefits

One benefit in using a competency approach for strengths development is that the breadth of each talent theme can be narrowed down to a more discrete level to see where growth opportunities exist. For example, consider that the talent theme of Communication includes the competencies of Verbal Communication, Nonverbal Communication, Listening, Facilitation, and Writing. Perhaps the student excels at Verbal Communication but is not as adept at Nonverbal Communication. By enhancing the competency of Nonverbal Communication, that student might be able to develop the talent theme of Communication into a strength.

In addition, for campuses already using strengths, integrating a competency approach can intentionally provide a way to assist students in developing their talents into strengths, providing the next step beyond strengths awareness. Integrating competency enhancement into strengths education can help educators develop intentional curriculum that can contribute to strengths development and use measurements to assess growth.

Although strengths-based programs are used across campuses in a variety of settings, linking leadership competencies to strengths development highlights the extent leadership can play a role in student success, academic achievement, and social integration. Leadership development is not just good for leadership; it is potentially good for persistence, success, and graduation. In addition, as colleges continue to market their value to incoming students, the commitment to developing leadership capacity is both a strong recruitment message and a great differentiator for students in college selection.

Finally, in addition to the value of using competencies for strengths development for individual students, there is a great benefit for educators, as they could intentionally design developmental experiences around competencies prevalent across many students' personal competency lists. For example, several students might have the competency of Other Perspectives on their personal competency lists because they have at least one of the Gallup, Inc. (2012) talent themes in which Other Perspectives is associated: Adaptability, Deliberative, Empathy, Ideation, Individualization, Input, Intellection, Learner, or Maximizer. Thus, the educator could offer a learning experience around the competency of Other Perspectives that would contribute to developing students' various associated talent themes into strengths.

NEW DIRECTIONS FOR STUDENT LEADERSHIP • DOI: 10.1002/yd

Limitations and Future Research

There are some limitations to this process. First, mapping competencies to talent themes only offers a framework. There is no empirical evidence that developing particular competencies makes a talent a strength. This article puts forth one process that may be helpful for leadership educators in designing curriculum and experiences that expose students to leadership competency development for the purpose of developing their strengths. Future research could include testing this process to see if, and to what extent, enhancing specific competencies develops associated strengths.

Second, some talent themes are listed as both a talent theme and a competency, perhaps leading to confusion about how they can both have the same or a similar name with one serving as the foundation for the other. This occurs with Analytical and Analysis, Empathy and Empathy, Ideation and Idea Generation, Includer and Inclusion, and Positivity and Positive Attitude. To clarify the difference, though, talents are innate, natural inclinations (Clifton, Anderson, & Schreiner, 2006), whereas competencies include learnable knowledge and skills (Seemiller, 2013). For example, Empathy as a talent theme would reflect someone's natural inclination to be empathic. The competency of Empathy, on the other hand, refers to demonstrating empathic behavior even if one might not be an empathic person. As noted in Table 3.1, there are many competencies associated with the talent theme, Empathy, beyond solely the competency of Empathy. This demonstrates the complexity and depth of an innate quality over a learned competency. Despite this clarification, semantics may create confusion in using both strengths and competencies, and learning the difference between the two would be helpful in their dual application.

Finally, there may be additional leadership competencies outside of the list of the 60 Student Leadership Competencies (Seemiller, 2013) associated with each talent theme. The list of competencies used in this chapter was selected based on it being an established framework grounded in research. Institutions already using the Student Leadership Competencies (Seemiller, 2013) and/or StrengthsQuest™ could easily use this content, however, other frameworks could be mapped using the same process as described in this chapter.

Conclusion

Helping students become aware of their talent themes can lead to many positive empirical outcomes (Louis, 2012). But, leveraging strengths is more than just about self-awareness; it involves building talents into strengths, which requires an intentional and developmental process. A leadership competency approach can offer a strategic map for moving beyond talent identification to holistic and cumulative strengths development.

NEW DIRECTIONS FOR STUDENT LEADERSHIP • DOI: 10.1002/yd

Notes

1. Strengths Portrait™ is a trademark of Total SDI, Carlsbad, CA.

2. Gallup®, Clifton StrengthsFinder®, StrengthsFinder®, the thirty-four Clifton StrengthsFinder theme names, StrengthsQuest™, and Clifton StrengthsFinder Themes® are trademarks of The Gallup Organization, Princeton, NJ.

References

Bowers, K. M., & Lopez, S. J. (2010). Capitalizing on personal strengths in college. *Journal of College and Character, 11*(1), 1–11.

Buckingham, M. (2007). *Go put your strengths to work: Six powerful steps to achieve outstanding performance.* New York, NY: Free Press.

Buckingham, M., & Clifton, D. O. (2001). *Now, discover your strengths.* New York, NY: The Free Press.

Centre for Applied Positive Psychology. (2009). *R2 Strengths Profiler.* London: Author.

Clifton, D. O., & Anderson, C. E. (2002). *StrengthsQuest.* Washington, DC: Gallup, Inc.

Clifton, D. O., Anderson, C. E., & Schreiner, L. A. (2006). *StrengthsQuest* (2nd ed.). New York, NY: Gallup Press.

Clifton, D. O., & Harter, J. K. (2003). Investing in strengths. In K. S. Cameron, J. E. Dutton, & R. E. Quinn (Eds.), *Positive organizational scholarship* (pp. 111–121). San Francisco, CA: Berrett-Koehler.

Conger, J. A., & Ready, D. A. (2004). Rethinking leadership competencies. *Leader to Leader, 32*, 41–47.

Dweck, C. S. (1999). *Self-theories: Their role in motivation, personality, and development.* Philadelphia, PA: Psychology Press.

Elo, S., & Kyngas, H. (2007). The qualitative content analysis process. *Journal of Advanced Nursing, 62*, 107–115.

Ennis, M. R. (2008). *Competency models: A review of the literature and the role of the employment and training administration (ETA).* Washington, DC: U.S. Department of Labor.

Gallup, Inc. (2012). *Clifton StrengthsFinder® themes.* Retrieved from http://www.gallup.com/poll/166991/clifton-strengthsfinder-theme-descriptions-pdf.aspx

Gallup, Inc. (2015a). *Strengths-based curriculum for the first-year experience* [PowerPoint slides]. Washington, DC: Author.

Gallup, Inc. (2015b). *What is the difference between a talent and strength?* Retrieved from http://strengths.gallup.com/help/general/125543/difference-talent-strength.aspx

Hodges, T. D., & Clifton, D. O. (2004). Strengths-based development in practice. In P. Linley & S. Joseph (Eds.), *Positive practice in psychology* (pp. 256–268). Hoboken, NJ: Wiley.

Hollenbeck, G. P., McCall, M. W., & Silzer, R. F. (2006). Leadership competency models. *The Leadership Quarterly, 17*, 398–413.

Intagliata, J., Ulrich, D., & Smallwood, N. (2000). Leveraging leadership competencies to produce leadership brand: Creating distinctiveness by focusing on strategy and results. *People + Strategy, 23*(4), 12–23.

Komives, S. R., Lucas, N., & McMahon, T. R. (2013). *Exploring leadership* (3rd ed.). San Francisco, CA: Jossey-Bass.

Lopez, S. J., & Louis, M. C. (2009). The principles of strengths-based education. *Journal of College and Character, 10*(4), 1–8.

Louis, M. C. (2008). *A comparative analysis of the effectiveness of strengths-based curricula in promoting first-year college student success* (Doctoral dissertation). Available from from Dissertation Abstracts International, 69(06A). (UMI No. AAT 3321378)

Louis, M. C. (2011). Strengths interventions in higher education: The effects of identification versus development approaches on implicit self-theory. *The Journal of Positive Psychology, 6,* 204–215.

Louis, M. C. (2012). *The Clifton StrengthsFinder and student strengths development: A review of research.* Omaha, NE: The Gallup Organization.

Mulder, M., Gulikers, J., Wesselink, R., & Biemans, H. (2008). *The new competence concept in higher education: Error or enrichment?* Paper presented at American Educational Research Association annual meeting, New York, NY.

Passarelli, A., Hall, E., & Anderson, M. (2010). A strengths-based approach to outdoor and adventure education: Possibilities for personal growth. *Journal of Experiential Education, 33,* 120–135.

Peterson, C., & Seligman, M. E. P. (2004). *Character strengths and virtues: A handbook and classification.* New York, NY: Oxford University Press and Washington, DC: American Psychological Association.

Posthuma, R. A., & Campion, M. A. (2008). Twenty best practices for employee performance reviews. *Compensation Benefits Review, 40,* 47–55.

Rath, T. (2007). *StrengthsFinder 2.0.* New York, NY: Gallup Press.

Robbins, C. J., Bradley, E. H., & Spicer, M. (2001). Developing leadership in healthcare administration: A competency assessment tool. *Journal of Healthcare Management, 46,* 188–202.

Schreiner, L. A. (2006). *A technical report on the Clifton StrengthsFinder with college students.* Retrieved from https://www.strengthsquest.com/Library/Documents/ SQwebsiteversionofvaliditystudy.doc

Seemiller, C. (2013). *The student leadership competencies guidebook: Designing intentional leadership learning and development.* San Francisco, CA: Jossey-Bass.

Seemiller, C. (2016). *Student leadership competencies inventory.* Retrieved from www.studentleadershipcompetencies.com

Sheldon, K., Frederickson, B., Rathunde, K., & Csikszentmihalyi, M. (2000). Positive psychology manifesto (Rev. ed.). Retrieved at http://www.sas.upenn.edu/ psych/seligman/akumalmanifesto.htm.

TotalSDI. (n.d.). *Strengths portrait.* Stamford, Lincolnshire, UK: Author.

Wright, K., Rowitz, L., Merkle, A., Reid, W. M., Robinson, G., Herzog, B., . . . Baker, E. (2000). Competency development in public health leadership. *American Journal of Public Health, 90,* 1202–1207.

COREY SEEMILLER *is a faculty member in the Department of Leadership Studies in Education and Organizations at Wright State University and was formerly the director of Leadership Programs at the University of Arizona. She has served as the co-chair for the National Leadership Symposium and co-chair for the Leadership Education Academy and is the author of* The Student Leadership Competencies Guidebook *and* Generation Z Goes to College.

4

This chapter provides recommendations for aligning instructional strategies with learning outcomes and leadership competencies to foster intentional student leadership development.

Aligning Instructional Strategies with Learning Outcomes and Leadership Competencies

Daniel M. Jenkins, Scott J. Allen

Leadership education can be defined as the pedagogical practice of facilitating leadership learning to build human capacity (Andenoro et al., 2013). Within this context, leadership learning involves "shifts in knowledge, behavior, personal insights, or consciousness as a result of educational experiences associated with the activity of leadership" (Allen & Shehane, 2016, p. 40) and serves as the desired outcome of leadership education in both curricular and co-curricular educational contexts (Andenoro et al., 2013). This chapter explores how leadership educators can more intentionally align instructional strategies with learning outcomes and leadership competencies to facilitate leadership learning through a five-step process.

A critical consideration of any leadership learning experience is to design with intentionality. Haber-Curran and Owen (2013) note that there are "leadership programs that lack purposeful frameworks, educational outcomes, and theoretical grounding" (p. 43). But, with an increased accountability within higher education and a need to engage in reflective and deliberative practice (Haber-Curran & Owen, 2013), leadership educators should approach the work ever-increasing levels of intentionality (Harper, 2011).

For leadership educators, it is essential to design with intention; more specifically, to plan and execute the design of curriculum and learning experiences to meet specified purposes (Wiggins & McTighe, 1998). Thus, if you can't describe why you have assigned a specific assignment or planned to facilitate a particular activity, you probably should not include it.

Instructional strategies help facilitate learning experience and can be defined as a set of tools (e.g., self-assessments, readings, and media), methods (e.g., discussion, reflection, role play, and activities), and content (e.g.,

NEW DIRECTIONS FOR STUDENT LEADERSHIP, no. 156, Winter 2017 © 2017 Wiley Periodicals, Inc., A Wiley Company
Published online in Wiley Online Library (wileyonlinelibrary.com) • DOI: 10.1002/yd.20270

theories, models, and competencies) that, when combined, create an instructional approach (Salas & Cannon-Bowers, 2001). Moreover, instructional strategies determine the plan for achieving learning objectives. They often align with the needs and interests of students to enhance learning and are based on many types of learning styles (Ekwensi, Moranski, & Townsend-Sweet, 2006). In this chapter, the term *instructional strategy* is synonymous with terms such as sources of learning, assignments, and classroom activities.

A review of the literature on the use of instructional strategies in leadership education offers only recent empirical data (see Jenkins, 2012, 2013). Nonetheless, there are several accounts of specific instructional strategies in practice such as reflection (Densten & Gray, 2001; Guthrie & Bertrand Jones, 2012), case study (Atkinson, 2014), service learning (Buschlen & Warner, 2014; Seemiller, 2006; Wagner & Pigza, 2016), self-assessments (Buschlen & Dvorak, 2011), role-play (Jenkins & Cutchens, 2012; Sogurno, 2003), and simulation (Allen, 2008). Relatedly, in his book *Learning to Lead*, Conger (1992) explored five innovative leadership training programs outside universities by being a participant and observer. After attending the various programs, Conger (1992) and his research team reported no "single best" approach for developing leaders. Instead, they found that each had distinct strengths and drawbacks and categorized leadership training into four approaches (later associated with "sources of learning" by Allen and Hartman, 2009). These include:

- Personal growth—training designed to improve self-awareness and overcome inner barriers to psychological growth and leader development (e.g., journal reflections and service learning).
- Conceptual understanding—improving the individuals' knowledge through exposure to the topic of leadership (e.g., case studies and articles or books).
- Feedback—processes through which individuals can learn about their strengths and weaknesses (e.g., assessments and instruments).
- Skill-building—leadership abilities that can be broken down into actual mechanical processes that participants can perform (e.g., simulations or games and role play activities).

Although each instructional strategy has benefits (Jenkins, 2012) and ideal contexts for implementation (Conger, 1992), might some be more suited for advancing student learning of particular competencies over others?

The Five-Step Design Process for Leadership Education

The following five-step process offers some clarity around leadership education design and accountability to ensure that instructors are utilizing instructional strategies that enhance students' leadership competencies while meeting the designated learning outcomes. This process provides both structure and intentionality for aligning instructional strategy choices with leadership competency development.

1. Identify learning outcomes and select desired leadership competencies: Begin with the end in mind. Backward design (Wiggins & McTighe, 2005) is critical to the effectiveness of any learning experience. What should students learn?
2. Select appropriate instructional strategies: The instructional strategies should align with the desired change in knowledge, values, abilities, and behaviors of the given competencies. How should students learn?
3. Consider situational factors: Assess the instructor's ability to deliver and facilitate learning with the chosen instructional strategies effectively. Likewise, assess the developmental readiness of learners (Thompson & Reichard, 2016), the learning environment, and the subject matter. What factors might impact student learning?
4. Design appropriate assessment measures: Integrate appropriate measurement tools for assessment of leadership competencies in each learning experience. How do we know learning has occurred?
5. Provide opportunities for evaluative feedback: Provide feedback related to leadership competencies selected. How do we help students reflect?

This five-step process can be used to design learning activities such as workshops, degree programs, courses, and one-time trainings. A review of the literature coupled with the research of Jenkins (2016b) suggests that various instructional strategies may be effective in teaching certain subject matter. For example, teaching ethics via simulation may be effective, but there is no research to support that it is a "best practice." Instead, we suggest there may be multiple effective practices.

Step 1: Identify Learning Outcomes and Select Desired Leadership Competencies.   The first step of this process includes identifying the desired learning outcomes. Learning outcomes are defined as "a stated expectation of what someone will have learned" (Driscoll & Wood, 2007, p. 5) and "descriptors of the intended results of educational activities" (Driscoll & Wood, 2007, p. 26).

After identifying a learning outcome, it is important to select specific leadership competencies associated with that learning outcome. The Student Leadership Competencies offers a list of 60 competencies that cut across four contemporary leadership models [Council for the Advancement of Standards in Higher Education (CAS), 2015], and the outcomes listed by 522 academic program accrediting agencies (Seemiller, 2013) and includes competencies such as personal values, conflict negotiation, verbal communication, initiative, and evaluation. See Chapter 3 for an identification of all competencies.

Once the competencies are identified, it is critical to determine what students need to know, believe, do, or develop each competency. Seemiller (2013) defines these four dimensions of competency development as:

- Knowledge: Knowledge of or understanding of a competency.
- Value: Value placed on a competency.
- Ability: Internal motivation to engage in a certain behavior or skill level to perform a certain behavior.
- Behavior: Engagement in a certain behavior.

The following example highlights how to use learning outcomes and competencies together.

- Learning outcome: Students will be able to articulate the four stages of group development.
- Associated competencies and dimensions: Group Development (knowledge).

Step 2: Select Appropriate Instructional Strategies. Leadership educators have a wide variety of instructional strategies from which to choose. For example, Hughes, Ginnett, and Curphy (2015) suggest integrating feedback, case studies, role-playing, and simulation into leadership studies programs, as these types of instructional strategies are "likely to contribute to development in a variety of ways" (p. 60). Moreover, instructional strategies share a capability to move learning from the cognitive to social and behavioral domains (Hughes et al., 2015) and provide a clear alternative to teaching as dispensing information (Bonwell & Eison, 1991).

Subsequently, it is critical to identify which instructional strategies effectively facilitate learning that meets the desired outcome(s) and aligns with competency development. There are two main approaches to doing this. First, the intended competency dimension (knowledge, value, ability, and behavior) may guide the selection of the instructional strategy. For example, what instructional strategies will best facilitate growth and development in knowledge, value, ability, and behavior for Verbal Communication? An effective instructional strategy to teach the knowledge dimension of verbal communication might differ from an effective strategy to teach the value dimension. Table 4.1 highlights a variety of instructional strategies aligned with associated competency dimensions.

The second approach to selecting instructional strategies is to consider that students may demonstrate outcomes or develop competencies simply by experiencing an instructional strategy regardless of the content. That is, leadership educators do not have to find a perfect instructional strategy to fit particular content, but more so that instructional strategies provide

Table 4.1   Instructional Strategies by Dimension

Instructional Strategy	Description	Examples	Associated student leadership competency dimension (Seemiller, 2013)
Case studies	Students examine written, digital, or oral stories or vignettes that highlight effective or ineffective leadership.	Harvard Case Study or Hartwick Classic Film Leadership Cases.	Knowledge; Ability
Discussion	Instructor facilitates sustained conversation and/or question-and-answer segment with the entire group.	Stimulating student-led discussion based on current events or case studies (Wisniewski, 2010).	Knowledge; Value; Ability
Debates	Student teams argue for or against a position using course concepts, evidence, logic, and so on.	Groups subdivided into teams–for and against current events or decision making.	Knowledge; Value; Ability
Games	Students engage in interactions in a prescribed setting and are constrained by a set of rules and procedures (e.g., game shows).	Prisoner's Dilemma (Gibson, 2003).	Knowledge; Ability
Reflection	Students develop written reflections on their experiences or understandings of lessons learned about content.	Written reflection activities in the form of journals or essays about readings; verbal reflection in reaction to class discussions; vision and goal-setting activities (Eich, 2008).	Knowledge; Value; Behavior
Role play activities	Students engage in an activity where they act out a set of defined role behaviors or positions with a view to acquire desired experiences.	Mimicking— demonstrative or illustrative of specific concepts, problems or situations (Sogurno, 2003).	Knowledge; Ability

(Continued)

Table 4.1   Continued

Instructional Strategy	Description	Examples	Associated student leadership competency dimension (Seemiller, 2013)
Self-assessments and instruments	Students complete questionnaires or other instruments designed to enhance self-awareness in a variety of areas (e.g., learning or leadership style, personality type).	StrengthsFinder (Rath, 2007); Leadership Practices Inventory (Posner & Kouzes, 1988); Myers-Briggs Type Indicator (Briggs-Myers & Briggs, 1985); Socially Responsible Leadership Scale (Tyree, 1998); and Emotionally Intelligent Leadership for Students: Inventory (Shankman, Allen, & Miguel, 2015).	Knowledge; Ability; Behavior
Service learning	Students participate in a service or philanthropic project.	Alternative breaks; site visits; volunteerism; and civic engagement.	Knowledge; Value; Behavior
Simulation	Students engage in an activity that simulates complex problems or issues and requires decision-making.	The StarPower Simulation (Allen, 2008).	Knowledge; Value; Behavior
Student peer assessment	Students critique other students' work using previously described criteria and provide specific suggestions for improvement.	Semester-long team project where students assess peers on their leadership competence, motivation to lead, and leadership self-efficacy (Rosch, Collier, & Zehr, 2014).	Knowledge; Ability; Behavior

(Continued)

Table 4.1   Continued

Instructional Strategy	Description	Examples	Associated student leadership competency dimension (Seemiller, 2013)
Team building	Students engage in group activities that emphasize working together in a spirit of cooperation (e.g., setting team goals/priorities, delegating work, examining group relation-ships/dynamics).	Collegiate Leadership Competition (Jenkins, 2016a); team-building courses.	Value; Ability; Behavior

learning and competency development in and of themselves. For example, using case studies can develop the competency of analysis just by going through the process of doing a case study, regardless of the topic of the case study. Table 4.2 outlines learning outcomes and competencies associated with participation in each instructional strategy.

All instructional strategies have pros and cons, and selecting the right instructional strategies can be challenging. The objective of this chapter is to encourage intentionality around the selection of instructional strategies and associated leadership learning outcomes and leadership competencies. The information in Tables 4.1 and 4.2 is grounded in a review of the leadership education literature and research focused on leadership educators' use of instructional strategies (Allen & Hartman, 2009; Jenkins 2012, 2013, 2016b) and the outcomes and competencies the authors believe are most closely aligned.

Step 3: Consider Situational Factors.   This step, borrowed from the work of Fink (2013) and his model of integrated course design, challenges leadership educators to consider contextual variables of the teaching and learning environment. These variables include the teaching and learning situation (e.g., the level of the course and/or program, delivery method, and institutional and/or curricular expectations), the nature of the subject (e.g., theory and/or practice), and the individual characteristics of the learners (e.g., traditional, first-generation, and graduate/undergraduate) and the instructor (e.g., experience teaching the course, subject, or modality). For example, over the last decade, universities such as the University of Southern Maine, University of Minnesota, and Azusa Pacific University have had multiple-year periods where utilization of the StrengthsFinder instrument was made an institutional priority in curricular and co-curricular settings.

Table 4.2   Outcomes and Competencies Associated with Instructional Strategies

Instructional strategy	Associated outcomes	Associated student leadership competencies (Seemiller, 2013)
Case studies	Provides situations, concepts, and images related to experiences students haven't yet had (Garvin, 2003; Parks, 2005).	Analysis, Others' Circumstances, Reflection and Application
Discussion	Model and understand empowerment and inclusive behaviors, listening, and communication (Cross, 2002).	Advocating for a Point of View, Appropriate Interaction, Listening, Verbal Communication, and Other Perspectives
Debates	Recognition of how values, assumptions, and principles affect practice; coordinating and delegating; shared decision-making; prioritization; and deep processing (Gould, 2012).	Verbal Communication, Listening, and Advocating for a Point of View
Games	Raise awareness, spark challenges, have normative implications, and are descriptive (Gibson, 2003).	Collaboration, Decision Making, and Problem Solving
Reflection	Learning from experience; increased locus of control; and open-mindedness (Dewey, 1933); active experimentation (Kolb, 1984); deeper learning and understanding (Densten & Gray, 2001; Guthrie & Bertrand Jones, 2012).	Self-Understanding, Personal Values, Self-Development, Reflection and Application, and Writing
Role-play activities	Reflective judgment (Jenkins & Cutchens, 2012); retention and theory to practice (Sogurno, 2003).	Verbal Communication, Nonverbal Communication, Other Perspectives
Self-assessments and instruments	Individual, group, and community values (Buschlen & Dvorak, 2011).	Reflection and Application, Self-Understanding, and Personal Contributions
Service learning	Community-based experiences related to course content (Buschlen & Warner, 2014; Seemiller, 2006); Critical thinking (Pascarella, Palmer, Moye, & Pierson, 2001); civic engagement; self-awareness; emotional intelligence; self-esteem; and self-efficacy (Webster, Bruce, & Hoover, 2006); and intersectionality (Stenta, 2001).	Service, Helping Others, and Social Responsibility

(Continued)

Table 4.2   Continued

Instructional strategy	Associated outcomes	Associated student leadership competencies (Seemiller, 2013)
Simulation	Skill demonstration (Allen, 2008) and globalization (Ewell, 2002).	Analysis and Problem Solving
Student Peer Assessment	Delegation; conflict negotiation; evaluation; and accountability (Buschlen, 2009).	Evaluation, Helping Others, and Providing Feedback
Team building	Exploring assumptions, engagement, participation, reflective learning, insight into others' values and their own, openness to differences, and increased self-awareness (Borredon, Deffayet, Baker, & Kolb, 2011).	Collaboration, Others' Contributions, Reflection and Application, Problem Solving, Other Perspectives

As a result, leadership programs at these institutions were expected to include learning activities that integrated students' StrengthsFinder results. Hence, contextual variables should inform decisions about what students can and should learn. See Chapter 3 to examine how to map leadership competencies onto strength themes.

Step 4: Design Appropriate Assessment Measures.   Assessment is the systematic basis for making inferences about and defining, selecting, designing, collecting, analyzing, interpreting, and using information to increase students' learning and development (Erwin, 1991). In effect, learning outcomes assessment may be used to clarify what students are gaining from the college experience and, perhaps of greatest importance, to measure the impact of leadership education on competency development. Making decisions about assessment involves critical considerations regarding the properties of evidence of student learning that include both authenticity and direct and indirect measures of that learning (Goertzen, 2013). To be authentic, assessment activities must "closely simulate or actually replicate challenges faced by adults or professionals" (Wiggins, 1998, p. 141). Per this distinction, outcomes deemed authentic are often valued at a higher level because of their proximity to the competency of interest (Ewell, 2002). Therefore, authentic assessment of learning will likely involve observable performance and provide opportunities for educators to acquire evidence of student learning based on direct measures.

Direct measures of student learning involve "observable deployment of the ability in question" (Ewell, 2002, p. 21) and include such strategies as oral presentations, demonstrations, case studies, and simulations among other approaches (Palomba & Banta, 1999). Goertzen (2013) stresses that direct measures of student learning may not be as authentic. However, direct measures of student learning are widely perceived as being more credible than indirect measures. Conversely, indirect measures of student learning usually capture affective reactions, testimonies, and consequences (e.g., reflection, self-assessments, job placement, civic participation; Goertzen, 2013).

In practice, authentic and direct forms of assessment within leadership education are multifaceted and encompass assessing leadership behaviors, learning outcomes, traits and styles, student needs and satisfaction, and attendance and participation (Owen, 2011; Roberts & Bailey, 2016). For instance, whether assessing the Social Change Model of Leadership Development (Higher Education Research Institute, 1996) or the Student Leadership Competencies (Seemiller, 2013), it is likely that a multidimensional approach will be needed to assess a competency such as Self-Understanding. Or, when measuring the four dimensions of the Student Leadership Competencies (Seemiller, 2013), a number of different assessment tools are needed to uncover attainment of desired knowledge, values, abilities, and behaviors. Perhaps easiest to measure is knowledge, which can be assessed by a traditional exam or test. Abilities may be assessed via rubric, skill sheet, checklist, or expert panel depending on how self-understanding is defined. Value could be assessed through a reflection paper or group dialogue (Allen & Shehane, 2016).

Step 5: Provide Opportunities for Evaluative Feedback.   Feedback may take many forms such as 360-degree feedback, peer assessment, self-evaluation, interactive logs with instructor responses, 1-minute papers, end-of-term surveys, individual reading/writing conferences, and action learning (Day, 2001; Fayne, 2009); and the feedback providers may include mentors, coaches, students, and teachers. If used effectively, feedback is an active learning process that challenges students to modify their personal theories of leadership (Wisniewski, 2010). For example, a structured and well-designed debrief of a role play can and should result in highly structured peer and instructor feedback on their performance (McEnrue, 2002). Accordingly, learners will relate new roles and behaviors to real-life situations, which prompt meaning making, a stronger retention of information, and more permanent learning (Sogurno, 2003). In any event, the instructor must look forward, beyond the time when the learning experience concludes, and ask the following question based on Fink's (2013) research: "In what kind of situation do I expect students to need, or be able to use, this knowledge?" Accordingly, opportunities for providing evaluative feedback happen in two primary domains: (a) as part of the leadership development process (i.e., actions and behaviors, versus evaluating content knowledge), and (b) as part of the dissemination of feedback to learners (i.e., emphasizing the importance of preparing leaders for feedback).

Accordingly, Larsen (1998) offers four strategies for instructors who want to help students become more conscientious users of feedback and develop feedback-seeking ability: (a) topic knowledge, (b) awareness of the feedback process, (c) cognitive modeling, and (d) practice in feedback-seeking behavior. For example, Step Five offers information about topic knowledge—in this case, feedback. If instructors begin a term or program with feedback as a subject, students can practice feedback use throughout the learning experience, hence, building awareness of the feedback process (knowledge). On cognitive modeling, if instructors model feedback giving, even drawing attention to their own practices, students become aware of the modeling (value). Instructors can provide opportunities for students to practice giving and receiving feedback with rubrics, one-on-one discussions, and group debriefs (ability). Finally, instructors can provide feedback through assignments and behavioral observation (behavior).

Discussion

The current state of the literature on leadership learning and education appears infantile when juxtaposed to other well-formulated professional areas. Moving forward, there are some ripe areas for further exploration as we collectively contribute to the research and practice of leadership learning and education: clarity around terminology, developing a practice field, and better supporting leadership educators.

Clarity Around Terminology.   Critical to the work outlined in this chapter is a need for clear and consistent definitions of key terms (e.g., leadership education, leadership learning), instructional strategies (e.g., case study, discussion), and domains of knowledge (e.g., CAS Standards). Although it may be unrealistic to believe that we can achieve consensus, there is a need for general agreement among scholars. By doing so, we can build a coherent and cohesive stream of quantitative and qualitative inquiry. At present, there is little cohesion among scholars around even the most basic concepts, and, thus, it is difficult to amass a foundation upon which to build. And although this chapter is not about terminology, we were confronted with this reality from the outset. How are we defining outcomes, leadership education, instructional strategies, and competencies?

The Practice Field.   Most leadership educators would agree that the vast majority of curricular and co-curricular leadership education is focused on conceptual understanding and personal growth activities. And although there is a degree of experiential learning, rarely does this learning lead to deep expertise (Ericsson & Pool, 2016). Critical to the work outlined in this chapter is an intentional eye on how to develop expertise in multiple domains (e.g., skill building, conceptual understanding, personal growth). When viewing leadership education through the lens of Conger's (1992) work, Allen and Hartman (2009) and Jenkins (2012, 2013) contend that conceptual understanding and personal growth opportunities prevail, and the intentional incorporation of leadership skill building and feedback (based on active experimentation) often lacks depth in the design of the learning. Although leadership skill building is often given a cursory nod, rarely is true skill developed in the context of a learning intervention. For instance, skills such as facilitating a problem-solving process, negotiation, navigating difficult conversations, critical thinking, and ethical decision-making might only be the focus of one or two sessions. There is an opportunity for leadership education to create a practice field, like what football players, chefs, and firefighters have in their professions, for students to put their knowledge into action.

The Role of Leadership Educators. When viewed "from the balcony" (Heifetz & Linsky, 2002, p. 66), the role of being a leadership educator is a tall order. Leadership connects closely to many topics such as psychology, sociology, communication, history, philosophy, political science, neuroscience, research methods, learning theory, and assessment. Likewise, from an instructional design standpoint, a leadership educator must have a great deal of skill, as was highlighted in this chapter. Not only does the individual need to have clarity regarding outcomes, but that person must also be skilled at delivering several instructional strategies depending on the intended learning outcomes or competencies.

Finally, because of the nature of the topic, many leadership educators work to model the process of growth and development for their students. There is a limited, but steadily increasing portfolio/catalog of resources, credentialing, and opportunities for leadership educators to build their own skills and abilities. There is a need for better support for leadership educators who might not have a background in instructional strategies.

Conclusion

Leadership education is an activity, and the instructional strategies are the drills, exercises, workouts, routines, and regimens of the practice field. Just like a football player may run routes, take snaps, or push a blocking sled down the field to develop and prepare for an upcoming game, students of leadership develop through the activity and experience of engagement in instructional strategies such as discussion, role play, reflection, peer assessment, and case studies. And, like football, instructors must be process-oriented and begin with the end in mind. Instructors must provide students a description of the intended learning and anticipated results of participating in the course or program. Moreover, instructors can explain to students why they have chosen particular instructional strategies for their learning experience, what may have informed their decisions, and the process through which they will assess learning and provide feedback. By aligning instructional design with leadership learning outcomes and competencies, leadership educators can offer a more sophisticated and intentional educational experience for learners.

References

Allen, S. J. (2008). Simulations as a source of learning: Using Star Power to teach ethical leadership and management. *Journal of Leadership Education, 7*(1), 140–149.

Allen, S. J., & Hartman, N. S. (2009). Sources of learning in student leadership development programming. *Journal of Leadership Studies, 3*(3), 6–16.

Allen, S. J., & Shehane, M. R. (2016). Exploring the language of leadership learning and education, *New Directions for Student Leadership, 151,* 35–49.

Andenoro, A. C., Allen, S. J., Haber-Curran, P., Jenkins, D. M., Sowcik, M., Dugan, J. P., & Osteen, L. (2013). *National leadership education research agenda 2013–2018: Providing strategic direction for the field of leadership education.* Retrieved from http://leadershipeducators.org/ResearchAgenda

Atkinson, T. N. (2014). The "reverse case study:" Enhancing creativity in case-based instruction in leadership studies. *Journal of Leadership Education, 13*(3), 118–128.

Bonwell, C. C., & Eison, J. A. (1991). *Active learning: Creating excitement in the classroom* (ASHE-ERIC Higher Education Report No. 1). Washington, DC: The George Washington University, School of Education and Human Development.

Borredon, L., Deffayet, S., Baker, A. C., & Kolb, D. (2011). Enhancing deep learning: Lessons from the introduction of learning teams in management education in France. *Journal of Management Education, 35,* 324–350.

Briggs-Myers, I., & Briggs, K. C. (1985). *Myers-Briggs type indicator (MBTI).* Palo Alto, CA: Consulting Psychologists Press.

Buschlen, E. (2009). *Can college students learn to lead? An examination of a collegiate leadership course using the social change model of leadership* (Doctoral dissertation). Available from ProQuest Dissertations and Theses database. (Publication No. AAT 3351998).

Buschlen, E., & Dvorak, R. (2011). The social change model as pedagogy. *Journal of Leadership Education, 10*(2), 38–56.

Buschlen, E. L., & Warner, C. A. (2014). "We're not in Kansas anymore" disaster relief, social change leadership, and transformation. *Journal of Student Affairs Research and Practice, 51,* 311–322.

Conger, J. (1992). *Learning to lead: The art of transforming managers into leaders.* San Francisco, CA: Jossey-Bass.

Council for the Advancement of Standards in Higher Education. (2015). *CAS professional standards for higher education* (9th ed.). Washington, DC: Author.

Cross, K. P. (2002). *The role of class discussion in the learning-centered classroom* (The Cross Papers No. 6). Phoenix, AZ: League for Innovation in the Community College and Educational Testing Service.

Day, V. D. (2001). Leadership development: A review in context. *Leadership Quarterly, 11,* 581–613.

Densten, I. L., & Gray, J. H. (2001). Leadership development and reflection: What is the connection? *The International Journal of Educational Management, 15,* 119–124.

Dewey, J. (1933). *How we think: A restatement of the relation of reflective thinking to the educative process.* Boston, MA: Houghton Mifflin Company.

Driscoll, A., & Wood, S. (2007). *Developing outcomes-based assessment for learner-centered education: A faculty introduction.* Sterling, VA: Stylus Publishing.

Eich, D. (2008). A grounded theory of high-quality leadership programs: Perspectives from student leadership development programs in higher education. *Journal of Leadership & Organizational Studies, 15,* 176–187.

Ekwensi, F., Moranski, J., & Townsend-Sweet, M., (2006). *E-Learning concepts and techniques.* Bloomsburg University of Pennsylvania's Department of Instructional Technology. Retrieved from http://iit.bloomu.edu/Spring2006_eBook_files/ebook_spring2006.pdf

Ericsson, A., & Pool, R. (2016). *Peak: Secrets from the new science of expertise.* New York, NY: Houghton Mifflin.

Erwin, T. D. (1991). *Assessing student learning and development: A guide to the principles, goals, and methods of determining college outcomes.* San Francisco, CA: Jossey-Bass.

Ewell, P. (2002). *Applying learning outcomes concepts to higher education: An overview.* National Center for Higher Education Management Systems (NCHEMS). Retrieved from https://www.cetl.hku.hk/wp-content/uploads/2016/08/OBA_1st_report.pdf

Fayne, H. R. (2009). Using integrated course design to build student communities of practice in a hybrid course. *New Directions for Teaching and Learning, 119,* 53–59.

Fink, L. D. (2013). *Creating significant learning experiences: An integrated approach to designing college courses* (2nd ed.). San Francisco, CA: Jossey-Bass.

Garvin, D. A. (2003, September–October). Making the case. *Harvard Magazine, 106*(1) Retrieved from http://academico.direito-rio.fgv.br/ccmw/images/7/72/Making_the_case.pdf

Gibson, K. (2003). Games students play: Incorporating the prisoner's dilemma in teaching business ethics. *Journal of Business Ethics, 48*(1), 53–64.

Goertzen, B. J. (2013). Assessment adrift: Review of the current state of assessment of academically based leadership education programs. *Journal of Leadership Studies, 6*(3), 55–60.

Gould, J. (2012). *Learning theory and classroom practice in the lifelong learning sector* (2nd ed.). London, England: Sage.

Guthrie, K. L., & Bertrand Jones, T. B. (2012). Teaching and learning: Using experiential learning and reflection for leadership education. *New Directions for Student Services, 140,* 53–63. San Francisco, CA: Jossey-Bass.

Haber-Curran, P., & Owen, J. E. (2013). Engaging the whole student: Student affairs and the national leadership education research agenda. *Journal of Leadership Education, 12*(3), 38–50.

Harper, S. R. (2011). Strategy and intentionality in practice. In J. H. Schuh, S. R. Jones, & S. R. Harper (Eds.), *Student services: A handbook for the profession* (5th ed., pp. 287–302). San Francisco, CA: Jossey-Bass.

Heifetz, R. A., & Linksy, M. (2002, June). A survival guide for leaders. *Harvard Business Review, 80*(6), 65–74. Retrieved from https://hbr.org/2002/06/a-survival-guide-for-leaders

Higher Education Research Institute. (1996). *A social change model of leadership development: Guidebook version III.* College Park, MD: National Clearinghouse for Leadership Programs.

Hughes, R. L., Ginnett, R. C., & Curphy, G. J. (2015). *Leadership: Enhancing the lessons of experience* (8th ed.). New York, NY: McGraw-Hill.

Jenkins, D. (2016a, October). Collegiate leadership competition: Past, present, and future. International Leadership Association—Member Connector. Retrieved from http://www.ila-net.org/members/directory/downloads/newsletter/8-2016Member Connector.pdf

Jenkins, D. (2016b). Relation of leadership educators' perceived learning goals and assessment strategy use. Proceedings of the 2016 Association of Leadership Educators Conference, 439–457. Retrieved from http://www.leadershipeducators.org/resources/Documents/Annual%20Conference% 20Proceedings%202016.pdf

Jenkins, D. M. (2012). Exploring signature pedagogies in undergraduate leadership education. *Journal of Leadership Education, 11*(1), 1–27.

Jenkins, D. M. (2013). Exploring instructional strategies in student leadership development programming. *Journal of Leadership Studies, 6*(4), 48–62.

Jenkins, D. M., & Cutchens, A. B. (2012). From theory to practice: Facilitating innovative experiential leadership theory-based role play activities. *Proceedings of the*

2012 Association of Leadership Educators Conference (pp. 256–262). Retrieved from http://leadershipeducators.org/Resources/Documents/2012%20ALE%20Conference%20Proceedings.pdf

Kolb, D. (1984). *Experiential learning: Experience as the source of learning and development*. Upper Saddle River, NJ: Prentice Hall.

Larsen, E. (1998). Feedback: Multiple purposes for management classrooms. *Journal of Management Education, 22*, 49–62.

McEnrue, M. P. (2002). Managerial skills teaching: Ten questions and twelve answers. *Journal of Management Education, 26*, 648–670.

Owen, J. E. (2011). Assessment and evaluation of leadership. In S. R. Komives, J. Dugan, J. E. Owen, C. Slack, & W. Wagner (Eds.), *The handbook for student leadership development* (2nd ed., pp. 177–202). San Francisco, CA: Jossey-Bass.

Palomba, C. A., & Banta, T. W. (1999). *Assessment essentials: Planning, implementing, and improving assessment in higher education*. San Francisco, CA: Jossey-Bass.

Parks, D. S. (2005). *Leadership can be taught*. Boston, MA: Harvard Business School Press.

Pascarella, E., Palmer, B., Moye, M., & Pierson, C. (2001). Do diversity experiences influence the development of critical thinking? *Journal of College Student Development, 42*, 257–271.

Posner, B. Z., & Kouzes, J. M. (1988). Development and validation of the Leadership Practices Inventory. *Educational and Psychological Measurement, 48*, 483–496.

Rath, T. (2007). *Strengthsfinder 2.0*. New York, NY: Gallup Press.

Roberts, D., & Bailey, K. (Eds.). (2016). *New Directions for Student Leadership, 151*.

Rosch, D. M., Collier, D. A., & Zehr, S. M. (2014). Self-vs.-teammate assessment of leadership competence: The effects of gender, leadership self-efficacy, and motivation to lead. *Journal of Leadership Education, 5*(1), 26–38.

Salas, E., & Cannon-Bowers, J. A. (2001). The science of training: A decade of progress. *Annual Review of Psychology, 52*, 471–499.

Seemiller, C. (2006). Impacting social change through service learning in an introductory leadership course. *Journal of Leadership Education, 5*(2), 42–49.

Seemiller, C. (2013). *The student leadership competencies guidebook*. San Francisco, CA: Jossey-Bass.

Shankman, M. L., Allen, S. J., & Miguel, R. (2015). *Emotionally intelligent leadership for students: Inventory*. San Francisco, CA: Jossey-Bass.

Sogurno, O. A. (2003). Efficacy of role-playing pedagogy in training leaders: Some reflections. *Journal of Management Development, 23*, 355–371.

Stenta, D. A. (2001). *The Mount Leadership Society: Promoting intersections of leadership and social change in a service-learning class*. (Doctoral dissertation). From ProQuest Dissertations & Theses database. (Publication No. AAT 3022577)

Thompson, S. E., & Reichard, R. J. (2016). Context matters: Support for leader developmental readiness. *New Directions for Student Leadership, 2016*(149), 97–104.

Tyree, T. (1998). Designing an instrument to measure socially responsible leadership using the social change model of leadership development. *Dissertation Abstracts International, 59*(06), 1945. (UMI No. 9836493)

Wagner, W., & Pigza, J. (Eds.). (2016). *New Directions for Student Leadership, 150*.

Webster, N. S., Bruce, J. A., & Hoover, T. S. (2006). Understanding the perceptions of service learning with teen leaders. *Journal of Leadership Education, 5*(1), 26–38.

Wiggins, G. (1998). *Educative assessment: Designing assessments to inform and improve student performance*. San Francisco, CA: Jossey-Bass.

Wiggins, G., & McTighe, J. (1998). *Understanding by design*. Alexandria, VA: Association for Supervision and Curriculum Development.

Wiggins, G., & McTighe, J. (2005). *Understanding by design* (2nd ed.). Alexandria, VA: Association for Supervision and Curriculum Development.

Wisniewski, M. A. (2010). Leadership and the millennials: Transforming today's technological teens into tomorrow's leaders. *Journal of Leadership Education, 9*(1), 53–68.

DANIEL M. JENKINS is associate professor and director of Leadership & Organizational Studies at the University of Southern Maine.

SCOTT J. ALLEN is associate professor of management at John Carroll University, where he teaches courses in leadership, management skills, and executive communication.

5

This chapter provides an overview of how a leadership competency approach grounded in emotional and social intelligence can help educators promote career readiness for students. Strategies and approaches for building leadership competencies will be reviewed.

Using Leadership Competencies as a Framework for Career Readiness

Anita R. Howard, Suzanne L. Healy, Richard E. Boyatzis

Early development of leadership competencies related to emotional and social intelligence (ESI) has been shown to enhance career learning, readiness, and success. Effective use of ESI leadership competencies has been linked to higher levels of employee engagement (Shuck & Herd, 2012), augmented job performance and career advancement (Kunnanatt, 2008), and increased career decision-making ability and positive employment experiences in young adults (Erford & Crockett, 2012; Puffer, 2011). Recognition that ESI is an essential element of leadership has sparked intensified interest in the demonstration of ESI by people at different levels of leadership in diverse career arenas (Morehouse, 2007). Competency-based approaches to ESI and leadership have been used to cultivate high potential managers (Cherniss, Grimm, & Liautaud, 2010; Dries & Pepermans, 2007); identify competencies that predict high performance and where/when these competencies are developed along a manager's career-life path (Dreyfus, 2008); and build a conceptual framework for leadership development in human resource development (Shuck & Herd, 2012).

A growing body of research has further demonstrated that effortful, sustained competency-building courses, and development programs have enabled participants in educational and workplace settings to enrich their leadership competencies, career readiness, and career engagement (Boyatzis, Lingham, & Passarelli, 2010; DiFabio & Kenny, 2011; Webb, 2009). If effortful investment in ESI-based leadership competency development fosters heightened career readiness and performance, what approaches can learners and educators take to make this investment?

NEW DIRECTIONS FOR STUDENT LEADERSHIP, no. 156, Winter 2017 © 2017 Wiley Periodicals, Inc., A Wiley Company
Published online in Wiley Online Library (wileyonlinelibrary.com) • DOI: 10.1002/yd.20271

Developing the Whole Person to Be Effective

Knowledge is necessary for job effectiveness, but knowledge alone is not sufficient. A person has to be able to use the knowledge. This capability emerges in the form of behavioral characteristics called competencies, which Boyatzis (2009a) defines as "the underlying characteristics of a person that lead to or cause effective or outstanding performance" (p. 750).

Competencies are the behavioral level of emotional intelligence (Boyatzis, 2009a; Cherniss & Boyatzis, 2013) and have empirically been shown to cause or predict outstanding leader, manager, or professional performance (Amdurer, Boyatzis, Saatcioglu, Smith, & Taylor, 2014; Boyatzis, 1982; Druskat, Mount, & Sala, 2005; Luthans, Hodgetts, & Rosenkrantz, 1988). Conceptual syntheses have also shown the relationship of competencies to effectiveness (Campbell, Dunnette, Lawler, & Weick, 1970; Goleman, 1998; Spencer & Spencer, 1993).

Competencies That Predict Leadership Effectiveness. The behavioral capabilities that predict leadership effectiveness include emotional intelligence competencies such as Emotional Self-Control and Adaptability; social intelligence competencies such as Teamwork, Empathy, and Influence; and cognitive competencies, such as Systems Thinking and Pattern Recognition.

The integrated concept of emotional intelligence competencies (EI) and social intelligence competencies (SI) provides a useful framework for identifying learned capabilities that result in outstanding or effective performance at work and in life (Boyatzis, 2009b). An emotional intelligence competency (EI) can be described as "an ability to recognize, understand and use emotional information about oneself that leads to or causes effective or superior performance" (Boyatzis, 2009a, p. 757). Similarly, a social intelligence competency (SI) can be described as "the ability to recognize, understand and use emotional information about others that leads to or causes effective or superior performance" (Boyatzis, 2009a, p. 757). Cognitive competencies can be described as the ability to perceive themes or patterns in seemingly random events (pattern recognition) and the ability to see multiple cause-and-effect relationships in complex phenomena (systems thinking; Boyatzis, Goleman, and Hay Group Inc., 2001/2007). Cognitive competencies are viewed as "threshold" competencies, because they are needed for adequate performance. However, they are not included in the integrated concept of ESI because their increased use does not necessarily lead to outstanding or effective performance.

The emotional, social, and cognitive intelligence competencies (Boyatzis, 2009a) are presented in the Emotional and Social Competency Inventory (ESCI) and Emotional and Social Competence Inventory, University version (ESCI-U), developed by Boyatzis and Goleman (1996) and Boyatzis et al. (2001/2007).

Causal Link Between ESI and Leadership Effectiveness. Longitudinal empirical studies on competency development have established that ESI competencies shown to distinguish effective and outstanding managers, leaders, and professionals can be developed in adults. These ESI competencies are presented in Table 5.1.

Table 5.1   The EI, SI, and Cognitive Intelligence Competencies

Cluster	Competency	Definition
Emotional intelligence competencies (EI)		
Self-awareness cluster	Emotional Self-Awareness	Knowing one's internal states, preferences, resources, intuitions
Self-management cluster	Emotional Self-Control	Keeping disruptive emotions in check
	Adaptability	Flexibility in handling change
	Achievement Orientation	Striving to improve or meeting a standard of excellence
	Positive Outlook	Seeing the positive aspects of things and the future
Social intelligence competencies (SI)		
Social-awareness cluster	Empathy	Sensing others' feelings and perspectives; taking an active interest in their concerns
	Organizational Awareness	Reading a group's emotional currents and power relationships
Relationship-management cluster	Coach and Mentor	Sensing others' development needs and bolstering their abilities
	Inspirational Leadership	Inspiring and guiding individuals and groups
	Influence	Wielding effective tactics for persuasion
	Conflict Management	Negotiating and resolving disagreements
	Teamwork	Working with others toward shared goals; creating synergy in pursuing collective goals
Cognitive intelligence competencies		
	Systems Thinking	Perceiving multiple causal relationships in understanding phenomena or events
	Pattern Recognition	Perceiving themes or patterns in seemingly random items, events, or phenomena

From the *Emotional and Social Intelligence Competency Inventory*, R. E. Boyatzis, D. Goleman, & Hay Group, Inc., 2001.

A longitudinal study on ESI competency development in an MBA program over 16 annual cohorts (Boyatzis, Passarelli, & Wei, 2014) examined the patterns of change and sustainability in students' gains in ESI and threshold cognitive competencies; the program featured five elements that promoted competency development (pp. 20–21):

1. A course on Leadership Assessment and Development (LEAD) using Intentional Change Theory (ICT) as the basis for design (Boyatzis & Saatcioglu, 2008; Goleman, Boyatzis, & McKee, 2002). Course design focused on developing the "whole person" and also four benchmarks, including completion of (a) a personal vision, (b) a personal balance sheet (identifying personal strengths, areas for improvement), (c) coaching sessions with a leadership coach, and (d) a learning agenda (creating a personal plan for leadership development; Boyatzis et al., 2010; Leonard, 2007).
2. An explicit shift to a philosophy of experiential learning and applied pedagogy (Kolb, 1984; Kolb & Kolb, 2011; Lingham, 2008).
3. A focus on specific competencies in selected courses while addressing course materials (e.g., a marketing course that assessed students on their presentation skills).
4. Required participation in field projects (i.e., group work and peer collaboration on projects in real life companies, organizations, and workplaces).
5. Opportunities to participate in voluntary activities such as marketing clubs.

This research documented strong and dramatic improvement among MBA students on demonstrated emotional, social, and cognitive intelligence competencies—and an overall history of successful competency development in studied cohorts.

A different longitudinal study on the long-term impact of ESI competency development on career satisfaction and success in cohorts from the same MBA program 5–19 years after graduation found that emotional, social, and cognitive competencies assessed at graduation predicted subsequent career satisfaction and success (Amdurer et al., 2014)—again showing that ESI leadership competencies can be developed and learned.

An Approach to Developing Competencies That Promote Career Readiness

Intentional Change Theory (ICT) is a useful framework for helping learners develop ESI competencies designed to prepare them for career readiness and success. The ICT framework describes the process of sustained competency development and change at multiple levels, that is, the individual, dyad, team, organization, community, and country levels (Boyatzis, 1982; Goleman et al., 2002). It explains how educators can help students identify a desired vision or purpose, convert it into a learning agenda, practice new approaches and behaviors, and build resonant relationships that support development and change. ICT includes five specific phases or "discoveries" that assist desired, sustained change: (a) the Ideal Self, (b) the Real Self, (c) the Learning Plan, (d) Experimentation and Practice with new behaviors, and (e) Trusting Relationships that support learning and development.

Competency development and sustained change can be achieved through iterative cycles of these phases. The ICT framework is presented in Figure 5.1.

Two emotional attractors or psycho-physiological states help people to work on the specific issues within each ICT phase and create the tipping points for movement from one phase to the next. These are the Positive Emotional Attractor/PEA and the Negative Emotional Attractor/NEA (Boyatzis, Rochford, & Taylor, 2015). The PEA relates to personal values, hopes, possibilities, strengths, and optimism that form our vision of what we most aspire to be and become. The NEA relates to present reality, requirements, problems, fears, and improvement needs that form our conception of what we are in everyday life (Howard, 2015). Iterative movement between the PEA and NEA supports learning and change that is personally authentic (i.e., moved by intrinsic motivation and interest) and also pragmatic (i.e., equipped to deal with extrinsic requirements, challenges, obstacles). In other words, people are more motivated, creative, optimistic, flexible, and resilient when learning, development, and growth are driven by their personal vision—and more able to solve problems, plan/prioritize, overcome obstacles, and address improvement needs through back-and-forth movement between the two emotional attractors (PEA-NEA).

Further, iterative movement between PEA and NEA reflects findings in neuroscience that show that individuals need to cycle between two different neural networks in order to solve problems, make decisions, learn new ideas, and work with people (Jack, Boyatzis, Khawaja, Passarelli, & Leckie, 2013): the Task Positive Network (TPN) and the Default Mode Network (DMN). When the TPN is activated, problem solving occurs (e.g., focusing on and addressing problems or tasks). However, being open to change efforts, developing new ideas, and growing leadership competencies occurs when the DMN is activated.

Another feature of the PEA and NEA is arousal of the hormonal systems of the sympathetic nervous system (SNS) and the parasympathetic nervous system (PNS). The SNS is the body's stress response and is inherently defensive. The PNS is the body's effort at renewal, activating the immune system, making it possible for neurogenesis to occur (i.e., the development of new neurons, which are the brain cells that receive, process, and transmit information to other cells in the body); and making it possible to be open to other people and emotions.

Overall, engaging vision/the PEA during intentional change, or when helping others to develop and change, is essential to promote thinking and creativity; openness to new ideas, people, and emotions; mind–body renewal; and activation of the DMN and PNS. Alternatively, focusing on current reality/the NEA promotes decision-making, problem solving, goal setting, performance, and activation of the TPN and SNS. Again, engaging vision/the PEA helps people to optimize learning, development, growth, and renewal—and counter the physiological and psychological harm done

Figure 5.1. Boyatzis' Intentional Change Theory
Adapted from Boyatzis (2009b). Reprinted with permission.

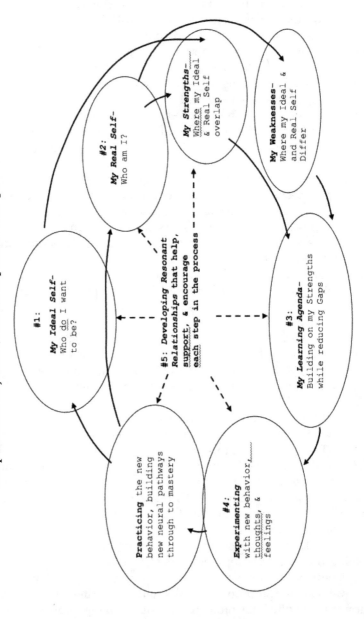

by work-related, performance-induced stress (McKee, Boyatzis, & Johnston, 2008). This awareness can help students and educators increase their understanding and use of the ICT framework for competency development.

In addition to ICT, Experiential Learning Theory (ELT) aids sustained competency development and change. As Peterson, DeCato, and Kolb (2015) describe

> ELT proposes that individuals grasp information through two dialectally opposed modes of Experiencing and Thinking, and may transform it into knowledge through Reflecting and Acting. When individuals use all four modes of the Learning Cycle [i.e., Experiencing, Thinking, Reflecting, Acting], they are able to experience an ideal, well-balanced learning process that keeps their subjective experience at the center of the learning (p. 230).

Using ELT to design a class, a course, and even programs can help to activate internal desires to learn, and do so effectively. Because people differ in learning style preferences, creating learning environments that appeal to all preferences for learning helps (Peterson et al., 2015).

How Do We Know It Works?   As previously discussed, longitudinal studies have established that adults can develop ESI competencies shown to predict management, leadership, and professional readiness and effectiveness, and this development sustains far longer than other forms of education or development (Boyatzis, Lingham, & Passarelli, 2010; Boyatzis & Saatcioglu, 2008; Boyatzis, Stubbs, & Taylor, 2002). These same competencies have been shown to predict life and career satisfaction as well as career success 5–19 years later (Amdurer et al., 2014). Thus, leadership competency development programs using ICT and ELT pedagogies hold significant promise for enhancing career readiness and success. What would a program using ICT and ELT pedagogies look like?

Using ICT and ELT Pedagogies to Promote Competency Development.   Students tend to be more excited about learning and more committed to practicing and using new knowledge and competencies when they have iterative opportunities to engage in personal learning and reflection through written exercises (e.g., writing a personal vision and learning plan, blogging or posting personal reactions to class readings and activities, keeping a personal journal about course learning and experiences, analyzing 360 feedback, reflecting on personal strengths and weaknesses, etc.), and applying what is being learned in current real-life settings (including written reflection on out-of-class experience and practice).

Using reflective exercises to engage learners through their emotions first and then helping them with the cognitive realizations is a powerful way to engage people. Then extending the stimulation into on-line discussion groups can create a basis for people to learn and help others through emerging relationships (Williams, Pesko, & Jaramillo, 2015). For example, robust learning communities and enhanced learning and engagement are promoted by interactive activities and exercises that help students form relationships, participate in peer coaching, work together on group projects, exchange ideas through online discussion boards and/or live chats with faculty, and form peer-facilitated learning circles or discussion groups (Baglione & Nastanski, 2007; Beckett, Amaro-Jimenez, & Beckett, 2010; Motsching-Pitrik, 2005; Walker, Curren, Keisler, Lammers, & Goldenson, 2013).

Inspiring Leadership Through an Emotional Intelligence Massive Open Online Course.   Building on previous years of experience and success in developing emotional (EI), social (SI), and cognitive intelligence competencies among MBA student cohorts, the authors, together with other program faculty members, developed a Massive Open Online Course (MOOC) on EI and leadership. Entitled Inspiring Leadership Through Emotional Intelligence (ILTEI) and offered through Coursera, the MOOC attracted roughly 187,000 participants from 205 countries in the first two runs of the course; by 2016, the MOOC had attracted over 582,000 enrollees from 215 countries, was being offered on demand and received recognition as one of the top two MOOCs worldwide.

The ILTEI MOOC featured nine classes, with three or so modules per class, to be taken over 6 weeks. Use of ICT and ELT was the basis for design, including a focus on the "whole person" and five benchmarks, including completion of (a) a personal vision; (b) personal learning assignments to reflect on and assess personal strengths, weaknesses, and so on; (3) action learning assignments to extend reflection, learning, and practice into daily experience; (4) practice coaching (i.e., written exercises or live peer coaching); and (5) weekly journal entries to promote integration of course concepts into career–life experience. In addition, weekly discussion forums were offered to foster peer engagement and a robust community of learning, and weekly quizzes provided individual feedback on mastery of course concepts.

The following framework used in the development of the ILTEI MOOC is rooted in ELT and designed to provide students with the opportunity to interact with the content and concepts in multiple ways, while encouraging development of a community of inquiry (deNoyelles, Zydney, & Chen, 2014; Kolb, 1976).

- Watch: Students are initially presented with one or more short videos introducing a new concept. The videos are intentionally kept to no longer than 15 minutes in order to encourage student persistence (Pomales-García & Liu, 2006). Guiding discussions with the use of prompts helps students to reflect more deeply on the content and provides a starting point for them to engage with other learners. This fosters a sense of community and encourages a higher level of cognitive presence (deNoyelles et al., 2014).

- Read: Students are provided recommended readings and supplemental readings that support and extend the new concepts presented in each module.
- Reflect: Reflective exercises provide an opportunity for students to examine their own beliefs and values more critically, and to assimilate new concepts into their daily personal and professional lives more easily (Meyers, 2008).
- Discuss: A discussion forum (i.e., an online discussion board) is built into each module, with specific questions or prompts provided by the instructor(s) to engage students in peer exchange about module content. Students are encouraged to share examples, ideas, and personal experiences that show their understandings and reactions to course concepts and content.
- Apply/Practice: Finally, students are provided with opportunities to engage in active experimentation that allows them to apply their burgeoning skills in authentic settings.

For the purpose of illustration, one module from the ILTEI MOOC is highlighted in Table 5.2, demonstrating the implementation of this approach.

Recommendations for Promoting Career Readiness. Using ESI-based leadership competencies as a framework for career readiness can be useful because it captures the essence of developing the whole person and drives sustained learning. Educators and learners can make a wise investment in competency development that increases career readiness, engagement, and performance through

- Early development of ESI competencies that lead to effective and outstanding performance.
- Creation of robust learning environments that engage students through their emotions, interpersonal relationships (e.g., peer learning and exchange, discussion groups, learning circles, etc.), active experimentation/practice, and personal reflections (e.g., reflective exercises, essays, journals).
- Approaches that employ ICT and ELT to support students for desired, sustained learning and change.

What we have learned from research and practice suggests that the most impactful learning will be supported by pedagogy that builds on both synchronous and asynchronous pedagogies as well as face-to-face methods with personal tutorials and peer coaching helping to expand learning retention. In addition, this pedagogy also holds the promise of reducing the costs of delivery.

Table 5.2   MOOC Activities Example

Module 1.1: What Is Great Leadership?	

Watch	What Is Great Leadership? -Professor Richard Boyatzis
	Course Introduction:
	    https://weatherhead.case.edu/media/videos/list/moocs/play/
	    mooc-emotional-intelligence
	Video Lecture:
	    https://echo360.org/media/f8b32268-648a-44d1-ab36-7f1
	    df1ef7c79/public

Read	Required Reading Goleman, D., Boyatzis, R., & McKee, A. (2001). Primal leadership: The hidden driver of great performance. *Harvard Business Review, 79*(11), 42–53. Recommended Readings Goleman, D., Boyatzis, R., & McKee, A. (2002). *Primal leadership: Realizing the power of emotional intelligence.* Boston, MA: Harvard Business School Press. McKee, A., Boyatzis, R.E. & Johnston, F. (2008). *Becoming a resonant leader: Develop your emotional intelligence, renew your relationships, sustain your effectiveness.* Boston, MA: Harvard Business School Press.
Discuss	How many leaders have brought out the best in you or not? What did they typically say or do? How did they make you and others feel?
Reflect	Think of the name of a leader you have worked with or for who brought out the best in you. Write their name on the top of the left hand column on a sheet of paper (or on your computer). This should be someone who was exciting to work with so much so that if they started a project in the community you would volunteer to work on it just to work with this person again. If they were head of another division of your organization, you would seek a transfer to be able to work with them. On the top of the right hand column, write the name of a leader with whom you worked that you try to avoid, someone who you thought was a lump. Remember the last few times you were around him or her, and underneath each person's name, reflect on the following questions: What did they typically say or do? How did they make you or others around them feel?
Apply/Practice	Quiz

Conclusion

According to the World Economic Forum's Future of Jobs Report (Leopold, Zahidi, & Ratcheva, 2016), emotional intelligence is a vital skill in today's fast-changing global employment landscape. Because of both the empirical benefits of developing emotional intelligence and the demand from employers for emotionally intelligent workers, using an ESI-based leadership competency approach with students can provide an effective way to develop and promote their career readiness and success.

References

Amdurer, R., Boyatzis, R. E., Saatcioglu, W., Smith, M., & Taylor, S. (2014). Long term impact of emotional, social, and cognitive intelligence competencies and GMAT on career and life satisfaction and career success. *Frontiers in Psychology*, *5*, 1–15. https://doi.org/10.3389/fpsyg.2014.01447

Baglione, S. L., & Nastanski, M. (2007). The superiority of online discussion. *The Quarterly Review of Distance Education*, *8*, 139–150.

Beckett, G. H., Amaro-Jimenez, C., & Beckett, K. S. (2010). Students' use of asynchronous discussions for academic discourse socialization. *Distance Education*, *31*, 315–335. https://doi.org/10.1080/01587919.2010.513956

Boyatzis, R. E. (1982). *The competent manager: A model for effective performance.* New York, NY: John Wiley and Sons.

Boyatzis, R. E. (2008). Leadership development from a complexity perspective. *Consulting Psychology Journal: Practice and Research*, *60*(4), 298–313. https://doi.org/10.1037/1065-9293.60.4.298

Boyatzis, R. E. (2009a). Competencies as a behavioral approach to emotional intelligence. *Journal of Management Development*, *28*, 749–770. https://doi.org/10.1108/02621710910987647

Boyatzis, R. E. (2009b). Leadership development from a complexity perspective. *Consulting Psychology Journal*, *60*, 298–313.

Boyatzis, R. E., & Goleman, D. (1996). *Emotional Competency Inventory.* Boston, MA: The Hay Group.

Boyatzis, R. E., Goleman, D., & Hay Group, Inc. (2001/2007). *Emotional and Social Competency Inventory.* Boston, MA: The Hay Group.

Boyatzis, R. E., Lingham, T., & Passarelli, A. (2010). Inspiring the development of emotional, social and cognitive intelligence competencies in managers. In M. Rothstein & R. Burke (Eds.), *Self-management and leadership development* (pp. 62–90). Cheltenham, United Kingdom/Northampton, MA: Edward Elgar Publishing.

Boyatzis, R. E., Passarelli, A., & Wei, H. (2014). Developing emotional, social, and cognitive competencies in MBA programs: A twenty-five year perspective. In R. E. Riggio & S. J. Tan (Eds.), *Leader interpersonal and influence skills: The soft side of leadership* (pp. 311–330). New York, NY: Routledge.

Boyatzis, R. E., Rochford, K., & Taylor, S. N. (2015). The role of the positive emotional attractor in vision and shared vision: Toward effective leadership, relationships, and engagement. *Frontiers in Psychology*, *6*, 1–13. https://doi.org/10.3389/fpsyg.2015.00670

Boyatzis, R. E., & Saatcioglu, A. (2008). A twenty-year view of trying to develop emotional, social and cognitive intelligence competencies in graduate management education. *Journal of Management Development*, *27*, 92–108.

Boyatzis, R. E., Stubbs, E. C., & Taylor, S. N. (2002). Learning cognitive and emotional intelligence competences through graduate management education. *Academy of Management Journal on Learning and Education*, *1*, 150–162.

Campbell, J. P., Dunnette, M. D., Lawler, E. E., & Weick, K. E. (1970). *Managerial behavior, performance, and effectiveness.* New York, NY: McGraw Hill.

Cherniss, C., & Boyatzis, R. E. (2013). Leader interpersonal and influence skills: The soft skills of leadership. In R. E. Riggio & S. J. Tan (Eds.), *Building interpersonal skills in management programs* (pp. 53–72). New York, NY: Routledge.

Cherniss, C., Grimm, L., & Liautaud, J. P. (2010). Process-designed training: A new approach for helping leaders to develop emotional and social competence. *Journal of Management Development, 29,* 413–431. https://doi.org/10.1108/026217110110391916

deNoyelles, A., Zydney, J., & Chen, I. (2014). Strategies for creating a community of inquiry through online asynchronous discussions. *Journal of Online Learning and Teaching, 10,* 153–165.

DiFabio, A., & Kenny, M. E. (2011). Promoting emotional intelligence and career decision making among Italian high school students. *Journal of Career Assessment, 19,* 21–34. https://doi.org/10.1177/1069072710382530

Dreyfus, C. R. (2008). Identifying competencies that predict effectiveness of R&D managers. *Journal of Management Development, 27,* 76–91. https://doi.org/10.1108/02621710810840776

Dries, N., & Pepermans, R. (2007). Using emotional intelligence to identify high potential: A metacompetency perspective. *Leadership & Organization Development Journal, 28,* 748–770. https://doi.org/10.1108/01437730710835470

Druskat, V., Mount, G., & Sala, F. (Eds.). (2005). *Emotional intelligence and work performance.* Mahwah, NJ: Lawrence Erlbaum.

Erford, B. T., & Crockett, S. A. (2012). Practice and research in career counseling and development—2011. *The Career Development Quarterly, 60,* 290–332.

Goleman, D. (1998). *Working with emotional intelligence.* New York, NY: Bantam Books.

Goleman, D., Boyatzis, R. E., & McKee, A. (2002). *Primal leadership: Realizing the power of emotional intelligence.* Boston, MA: Harvard Business School Press.

Howard, A. (2015). Coaching to vision versus coaching to improvement needs: A preliminary investigation on the differential impacts of fostering positive and negative emotion during real time coaching sessions. *Frontiers in Psychology, 6,* 1–15. https://doi.org/10.3389/fpsyg.2015.00455

Jack, A. I., Boyatzis, R. E., Khawaja, M. S., Passarelli, A. M., & Leckie, R. L. (2013). Visioning in the brain: An fMRI study of inspirational coaching and mentoring. *Social Neuroscience, 8,* 369–384. https://doi.org/10.1080/17470919.2013.808259

Kolb, D. A. (1976). Management and the learning process. *California Management Review, 18*(3), 21–31.

Kolb, D. A. (1984). *Experiential learning: Experience as the source of learning and development.* Englewood Cliffs, NJ: Prentice Hall.

Kolb, A. Y., & Kolb, D. A. (2011). Learning styles and learning spaces: Enhancing experiential learning in higher education. *Academy of Management Learning and Education, 4,* 193–212.

Kunnanatt, J. A. (2008). Emotional intelligence: Theory and description. A competency model for interpersonal effectiveness. *Career Development International, 13,* 614–629. https://doi.org/10.1108/136204308109111083

Leonard, D. C. (2007). The impact of learning goals on emotional, social, and cognitive intelligence competency development. *Journal of Management Development, 27,* 109–128. https://doi.org/10.1108/02621710810840794

Leopold, T., Zahidi, S., & Ratcheva, V. (2016). *Global challenge insight report: The future of jobs—Employment, skills and workforce strategy for the fourth industrial revolution.* Cologny/Geneva, Switzerland: World Economic Forum.

Lingham, T. (2008). Experiential learning theory. In S. R. Clegg & J. R. Baily (Eds.), *International encyclopedia of organization studies* (Vol. 2: E-L; pp. 413–836). Thousand Oaks, CA: Sage.

Luthans, F., Hodgetts, R. M., & Rosenkrantz, S. A. (1988). *Real managers.* Cambridge, MA: Ballinger Press.

McKee, A., Boyatzis, R., & Johnston, F. (2008). *Becoming a resonant leader: Develop your emotional intelligence, renew your relationships, sustain your effectiveness.* Boston, MA: Harvard Business Press.

Meyers, S. (2008). Using transformative pedagogy when teaching online. *College Teaching, 56,* 219–224.

Morehouse, M. (2007). An exploration of emotional intelligence across career arenas. *Leadership & Organization Development Journal, 28,* 296–307. https://doi.org/10.1108/01437730710752184

Motsching-Pitrik, R. (2005). Person-centered e-learning in action: Can technology help to manifest person-centered values in academic environments? *Journal of Humanistic Psychology, 45,* 503–530. https://doi.org/10.1177/0022167805279816

Peterson, K., DeCato, L., & Kolb, D. A. (2015). Moving and learning: Expanding style and increasing flexibility. *Journal of Experiential Education, 38,* 228–244. doi: org/10.1177/1053825914540836

Pomales-García, C., & Liu, Y. (2006). Web-based distance learning technology: The impacts of web module length and format. *American Journal of Distance Education, 20,* 163–179. https://doi.org/10.1207/s15389286ajde2003_4

Puffer, K. A. (2011). Emotional intelligence as a salient predictor for collegians' career decision making. *Journal of Career Assessment, 19,* 130–150. https://doi.org/10.1177/1069072710385545

Shuck, B., & Herd, A. M. (2012). Employee engagement and leadership: Exploring the convergence of two frameworks and implications for leadership development in HRD. *Human Resource Development Review, 11,* 156–181. https://doi.org/10.1177/1534484312438211

Spencer, L. M., Jr., & Spencer, S. M. (1993). *Competence at work: Models for superior performance.* New York, NY: John Wiley and Sons.

Walker, K., Curren, M. T., Keisler, T., Lammers, H. B., & Goldenson, J. (2013). Scholarly networking among business students: Structured discussion board activity and academic outcomes. *Journal of Education for Business, 88,* 249–252. https://doi.org/10.1080/08832323.20212.690352

Webb, K. S. (2009). Why emotional intelligence should matter to management: A survey of the literature. *Advanced Management Journal, 74,* 32–41.

Williams, S. S., Pesko, J. D., & Jaramillo, A. (2015). Improving depth of thinking in online discussion boards. *Quarterly Review of Distance Education, 16*(3), 45–66.

ANITA R. HOWARD *is an adjunct professor and executive coach in the Department of Organizational Behavior, Weatherhead School of Management, Case Western Reserve University.*

SUZANNE L. HEALY *is director of Online and Hybrid Learning at the Weatherhead School of Management, Case Western Reserve University.*

RICHARD E. BOYATZIS *is a distinguished university professor in the Departments of Organizational Behavior, Psychology, and Cognitive Science at Case Western Reserve University.*

6

This chapter introduces gamification and a model for utilizing game design elements for leadership competency development.

Utilizing Gamification to Foster Leadership Competency Development

Adam R. Cebulski

Over the past few years, gaming has opened doors for advertisers, social networks, and even educators to engage students better. Every day, millions of students hunt for Pokémon on college campuses in hopes of becoming a Master Trainer. Pokémon Go launched on mobile devices in July of 2016, and within its first month, the app had more than 100 million downloads, with more than 20 million of those individuals logging in daily to play (Cranford, 2016). In years past, people harvested their crops on FarmVille and made their way through a sugar-coated environment in Candy Crush. The gaming industry has tapped into human motivation to create digital experiences that drive behaviors and increase engagement, capitalizing on motivation and incentive systems. Although academic research on gamification in nongaming contexts has increased dramatically over the past 6 years (Hamari, Koivisto, & Sarsa, 2014), there has been little inquiry into gamification's impacts on competency development. This chapter will introduce a model for integrating gamification principles in leadership education and provide insight into how intentionally designing programs with this model can enhance leadership development.

Human Motivation and Game Design

Self-determination theory, developed by Deci and Ryan (1985), posits that individuals are ever-evolving organisms who can thrive on challenges if given the appropriate environments. Their theory states that motivation and engagement are usually considered prerequisites for the completion of a task or encouragement of a specific behavior (Deci & Ryan, 2000). Self-determination theory outlines three innate psychological needs: autonomy, competence, and relatedness. Autonomy refers to students having the freedom to act independently and make their own choices within a given

NEW DIRECTIONS FOR STUDENT LEADERSHIP, no. 156, Winter 2017 © 2017 Wiley Periodicals, Inc., A Wiley Company
Published online in Wiley Online Library (wileyonlinelibrary.com) • DOI: 10.1002/yd.20272

context. Taking away control or limiting the choice students have in a situation can actually be demotivating. Competence refers to a student's perception that they have the ability or knowledge to complete a task or succeed in a situation. Challenges can be motivating, but if perceived to be insurmountable, they can negatively affect students' interaction with the game design elements. Finally, relatedness refers to the personal associations a student makes to the experiences. A student who can intellectually and emotionally connect to the experience is more likely to persist throughout the entire program, as opposed to someone who feels it is not a good fit with their values.

Framing and Defining Gamification

The widely used definition for gamification comes from Deterding, Sicart, Nacke, O'Hara, and Dixon (2011), and refers to adding game design elements to nongame situations. Often the intention of these applications is to make an experience more engaging and to make the user feel rewarded for participating in specific behaviors. Corporate reward programs are a great example of gamification. The more consumers exhibit behaviors such as purchasing drinks, the more reward points they build up until ultimately, they can redeem them for prizes, goods, or services. Gamification can be as high-tech as digital tracking and leaderboards to as low-tech as paper-tracking systems like those used in many traditional degree-completion worksheets.

Gamification in Education.   In the classroom, gamification is becoming a more common form of pedagogy. Although its use appears to be discussed more in the K–12 literature, the discussion of gamification in higher education seems to be emerging, including the integration of game design elements like badges for developing competencies in program-specific curriculum. It is important to note the difference between introducing game design elements through gamification and implementing game-based learning in an educational context (Isaacs, 2015). Gamification is not game-based learning, which is the actual use of games within an educational context; just the integration of game design concepts or principles within a given setting. The distinction is incredibly important in making sure programs are incorporating elements of game-based design instead of a program being designed to be a game itself. For instance, playing a trivia game in class is implementing a game into the classroom, while introducing elements like scoring or leaderboards is actually gamifying the experience without the entire experience being a game.

Some institutions are integrating gamification into retention efforts in an attempt to keep students more regularly engaged outside of the classroom (Raths, 2015). Techniques involve encouraging students to use technology to complete achievements and track progress toward co-curricular involvement through mobile apps, on-line progress trackers, and incentives.

Education Examples.   Elementary and secondary education have historically done a better job of integrating gamification into the classroom. Many adults today remember the gold stars they tried to earn in classes or the sticker charts marking progress toward completion of a goal. High school introduces students to degree planning, allowing them to choose electives to complete certain requirements around the arts, languages, and home economics-type classes. Additionally, higher education is integrating more game design elements into programming such as orientation in which offices are increasingly using mobile apps to engage incoming students during and after their on-campus events (Fitz-Walter, Tjondronegoro, & Wyeth, 2011). These offices offer everything from leveling up on an app as students complete tasks in different areas of campus, to adding social interest matching to other students matriculating that year. Each of these examples demonstrates the integration of game design elements into programs or services with the end goal of increasing engagement within an increasingly technologically savvy student body.

Designing the Gamified Leadership Competency Experience: A Four-Domain Model

Overall, a prevailing theme of research in gamification indicates the necessity to create a user-centered experience (Deci & Ryan, 2004; Deterding, 2011). There has been a wealth of research on why individuals play games and more importantly what factors continue to engage a user in a traditional gaming environment (Hamari et al., 2014; Yee, 2006). These same motivational patterns can then be applied to programs outside of game-based environments to engage individuals in a meaningful way. Naturally, programs aimed at developing leadership competencies in students have a similar desire to focus on the individual, but staffing, financial, or other resource limitations often make it hard to build as customized of an experience as research shows can be most impactful.

When embarking on program design around the integration of gamification with leadership competency development, a four-domain model should be considered to ensure gamification is intentionally and realistically implemented. The four domains are mechanics, elements, resources, and customization, and are illustrated in Figure 6.1. These domains individually and collectively address the motivation components outlined in the self-determination theory and align with the basic principles of Universal Design in Learning (Rose & Meyer, 2002). This model is designed for application to formal leadership programs or activities as described by Haber (2011) in The Handbook for Student Leadership Development. The model also shows how the four elements can work independently and in more cohesive ways depending on the structure of the leadership education

Figure 6.1.   Program Gamification Model

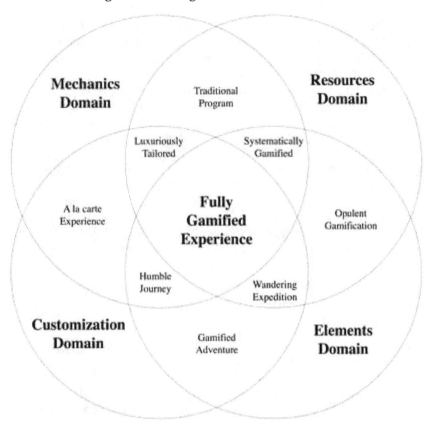

program and the resources available. Although the ultimate goal is to have a fully gamified experience, there are times where it may be more appropriate to focus more heavily on specific domains to achieve specific outcomes. The remainder of this chapter will describe each domain, domain interactions that can help students be successful, and potential challenges in focusing too heavily on a single domain.

Domain One: Mechanics

When we attempt to play a game, one of the first things we do is read through the rules to understand how the game is played and how it is won. In the gaming world, this concept is referred to as the mechanics of the game. Yee (2006) claims people have an inherent interest in understanding the rules of game play and the system by which they can optimize their performance under those rules. For leadership programs, it must be clear to students how they will be able to progress through the program including expectations of time, behaviors, and assessment as well as what situations they may encounter during the program. The mechanics domain specifically refers to a structured learning experience where students are given clear objectives toward developing leadership competencies. They understand what is expected throughout the program and how they will need to demonstrate achievement of the competencies. Often, curricular leadership education experiences focus heavily on the mechanics domain since much of the focus is dedicated to the curriculum and demonstration of knowledge acquisition as evidenced through a syllabus or program outline. Mechanics can also apply to things like bylaws for an organization; co-curricular programs might ensure that students attempting a campus policy change understand the rules of Campus Senate, including time lines and forms for presenting motions.

Game Structures and Motivation.   Yee's (2006) research on motivation in playing games revealed what was deemed the achievement component of motivation. A prime motivation in games is a desire to move forward in a game through gaining power, earning points, wealth, or status. Individuals want to know they are making progress within the mechanics of the game experience. Game progress most often directly relates to the game's scoring system. Individuals can become frustrated if they do not clearly understand how their score relates to their level within a game and particularly how that score needs to be changed to get to the next level. For students in leadership programs, students need to know where they are at concerning their progress at any given time. It may be as simple as students wanting to know if they are on track to complete the program, to as detailed as wanting to know how far they are from the next achievement, or their growth in competency levels perceived by themselves or by observers. Or in an actual change effort, students may need to celebrate small wins (Kotter, 1996) as they make progress, like getting a policy out of a committee and onto the Senate floor for action. Research has shown there is no significant correlation between the type of game progress elements used and success metrics or persistence rates for programs (Mekler, Brühlmann, Opwis, & Tuch, 2013). Administrators should choose a system that helps students be able to monitor their progress that makes the most sense based on the particular competency they are addressing or the composition of the students participating in their program.

Potential Pitfalls.   Focusing exclusively on the mechanics domain indicates a program is well structured but does not integrate any other game elements into the program design. Having only a scoring and tracking system places more emphasis on participation numbers and satisfaction evaluations than assessing the development of the competencies. Educators focusing primarily on this domain in their programs may find it challenging to keep students engaged on a longer-term basis and may rely heavily on extrinsic motivation, as students likely will want to move forward to check the completion box instead of personally connecting to the content.

Domain Two: Elements

The elements domain places the focus on choosing which aspects of game design are integrated into the pedagogical approach to competency development. Students may have a variety of opportunities to interact with game elements, like a leaderboard, visualizing who has achieved specific competencies, or the ability to receive badges after completing particular requirements for each competency. This domain allows for a very interactive and modern program, allowing administrators to tap into the technological aptitude of today's college student.

Scoring Elements.   One of the largest components in grasping how a game works involves clearly understanding the scoring system. Some games are simple, with a point system based on accomplishing tasks or performing specific actions. Others utilize a more complex scoring mechanism based on not only completing actions but also doing so in a particular sequence or within a specific time frame. If it is easy for users to understand the scoring system for a game, they might be more likely to want to continue to play. An example of scoring elements can include leaderboards, which are an easy way for users to see how they compare to others participating in the same experience. Often leaderboards are implemented to increase competition among players. This tactic can actually result in a decrease in motivation if it jeopardizes the competency component of the self-determination theory. Specifically, it can be very demotivating if an individual feels too far behind the leaders to catch up, resulting in programs running the risk of students lying or overinflating growth on developmental metrics in order to move forward artificially. This game element can also shift the experience from an intrinsic motivation of wanting to compete and fully immerse in the experience to an extrinsic motivation of only caring about the position on the leaderboard. Developing leadership competencies is specific to an individual, so if leaderboards are used, it must be clear they are not being presented to encourage competition but rather to show overall progress of all participants. Two keys to accomplishing this are to make sure the visualization shows all participants, and to ensure the leaderboard is not displayed in a way that puts those who are farther ahead (regarding progress) visually above those not as far along.

Achievements.   At their core, achievements are the milestones of participating in a gamified experience. They are what indicate progress and motivate players to continue through the experience. The most common forms of achievements are levels, unlockables, and badges.

Levels.   In gamification, levels can refer to the level of the individual or the environment in which they occupy during the experience. For leadership development, the focus needs to be on the level of the individual student. This concept can be reflected in staging different experiences, so they appear to build off each other and require the student to experience them sequentially.

Unlockables.   Unlockables refer to the ability to gain access to content or opportunities once a user reaches a particular score, position or rank in the experience, or after having completed an action. Similar to leaderboards, unlockables have the potential to shift motivation extrinsically as students may focus more on the unlockable itself rather than assimilating the learning inherent in the experience (Deci & Ryan, 2004). Unlockables need to remain meaningful to a student's experience within the context of the overall program. An example of an unlockable in a leadership program might be to be able to meet a prominent leader after achieving a certain level or completing a specific task. Unlockables should be rewards that students would not have access to on their own.

Badging.   One of the most common elements of gamification is the use of badges, which are visual representations of accomplishments in gamified environments. Badges are nothing new to experiential education – various scout groups have had badges for decades, essentially providing a physical patch to adolescents as they demonstrate competencies in a variety of skill areas. Badges can be thought of like the modern version of certificates often associated with the completion of learning activities. Mozilla Open Badges paved the way for universities and non-profit organizations to utilize electronic badges for learners of all ages (Raths, 2013). Electronic badges contain metadata describing the requirements the learner must pass in order to achieve the badge as well as information on who distributed it, when it was earned, and the exact criteria met for completion. Electronic badges are available through a wide variety of for-profit and nonprofit vendors like Credly, Open Badges, and Badge Alliance and link to ePortfolios, social media profiles, and personal websites.

Potential Pitfalls.   Programs only addressing the elements domain may seem very exciting like a game, but can lack a clear direction for the student whose focus may be on earning rather than learning. Another potential pitfall can occur when the program focuses too much on the game elements rather than being user-centered (Nicholson, 2012), meaning it becomes more about pushing students through the program for participation numbers than focusing on the actual competency development. Additionally, concentrating solely on this domain can diminish the intrinsic motivation students have for developing the competencies themselves. They will shift to an extrinsic motivation of getting to the top of the leaderboard or collecting all of the badges instead of reflecting critically on the experience and the completion of each dimension of the competencies.

Domain Three: Resources

The resources domain emphasizes having the staff, financial, or technological resources (among others) to implement a program addressing leadership competency development. Resources can include program funding, the expertise of professionals, pedagogical tools, technology integration, and other time-intensive work to make the gamified program a meaningful learning experience.

Potential Pitfalls.   Focusing too heavily on resources can lead to a program seeming flashy and exciting externally, yet participants may have trouble understanding the larger purpose of the program or how all of the resources available actually help them develop leadership competencies. Although it is great to commit resources to a program, it must be done in an intentional manner that complements all facets of program delivery and outcomes.

Domain Four: Customization

The customization domain focuses on ensuring the entire experience is student-centered. Gamification research has shown it is critical not to apply a cookie-cutter approach when integrating game design elements into non-game environments (Deterding, 2011; Nicholson, 2012). Goals can decrease motivation if the individual does not perceive them as personally relevant or meaningful. For example, if a leadership program is gamified to predetermine which competencies every student will achieve, but those particular competencies do not match a student's personal or professional aspirations, then there may be little intrinsic motivation to persist in the program.

In some cases, the extrinsic motivation of the reward may be enough to keep students, but they will not have long-term retention of the knowledge or skills gained in the experience. Ideally, programs helping students to develop leadership competencies would allow students to focus on particular competencies or category areas based on personal interests, career plans, or leadership roles. By allowing students to customize their experience, it ensures programs are looking at the three components of motivation, which are:

- Autonomy—the process in which students can identify their paths, like a choose your own adventure book.
- Persistence—students are more likely be intrinsically motivated when they are personally invested in particular competencies.
- Personal connection—having the customization allows them to value their competencies because they better understand the connection of why they were chosen, as would happen with career-based competencies.

For instance, programs using this domain as their foundation may allow students to choose specific leadership competencies related to their career aspirations or personal interests. The programs would need to be flexible enough to have an a la carte approach to learning, so students have the autonomy to build their own experience.

New Directions for Student Leadership • DOI: 10.1002/yd

Potential Pitfalls.   Too much emphasis on this domain can lead to programs having so much flexibility that it is hard to find a common theme or overall purpose for the programs. This may be evident in offering such a wide variety of leadership workshops, lectures, or classes they may seem like disparate events lacking a common purpose.

Domain Interaction and Intentional Design

Naturally, program design does not lend itself to falling solely within one domain of this model. Ideally, all domains are addressed, resulting in a fully realized experience successfully implementing game design elements for an intentional and deliverable program for students. While addressing all four domains is ideal to ensure programs meet all aspects of proper game design in the context of competency development, there may be situations in which some domains receive more attention than others. Intentionally limiting a domain is different than not taking it into consideration. As long as the limitation of a domain is intentional and aligned with the goals and outcomes of a particular program, the experience can be successful.

Traditional Program.   Traditional programs blend the mechanics and resources domains, but may lack in the elements and customization domains. These programs are likely the most prevalent in leadership education because much of the focus is around providing guidelines for how a competency is demonstrated and resources are committed to teaching and assessing outcomes. When mechanics are emphasized in leadership competency development, the student must clearly understand how they will be assessed against various dimensions for each competency (Seemiller, 2013). For instance, if a student is being assessed for the ability dimension of a particular competency, they must have a clear understanding of the expectations for completion. Often, this action is accomplished by providing students with a rubric for that particular dimension and competency. Programs focusing on particular competencies or addressing competencies specific to an occupation may intentionally limit the amount of customization available because they have a more concrete and standard set of outcomes students must achieve.

A La Carte Experiences.   Focusing on the mechanics and customization domains yields programs in which students have the autonomy to choose particular tracks or focus areas for their competency development. The most common form of this style of program is through offering an array of leadership education workshops among a variety of themes and requiring students to complete a certain number but allowing them the flexibility to choose the ones they will attend. The SUNY Geneseo GOLD program allows students to choose their own level of a leadership program, all of which are themed around precious gems and stones. Differing levels have a variety of expectations including time commitments and reflective activities. Curricular programs see this domain interaction represented through a similar process of requiring a certain amount of identified courses and allowing students to choose from the list. Programs just starting to integrate gamification may intentionally limit the number of game design elements they include, as these may require more advanced technical knowledge, or additional resources that may not be readily available.

Luxuriously Tailored. These programs seamlessly combine the mechanics and customization domains into a resource-rich learning environment potentially through implementing a more robust technological landscape to deliver the program such as a web- or mobile-based learning platform. Traditionally, these programs are seen in the curricular space because the institution has made a significant financial commitment to offering technology to support learning. Committing more resources to these programs moves them away from being a la carte toward more robust experiences that may have a more substantial theme and consistency to them.

Gamified Adventure. The gamified adventure is marked by the combination of the customization and elements domains. For students, it can be exciting to have a learning environment that encourages them to explore a variety of opportunities, experiences, and resources available on campus. This approach works by encouraging students to participate in activities of their choice and tracking their participation. At certain points, whether it is because they participated in a certain number of leadership development experiences or because they found a random "signature activity," they may gain access to particular experiences unlocked specifically for them. There must be mechanics behind unlockables with clear protocols for how they can be unlocked, or it must be entirely random. Unlockables can easily be demotivating if students feel like unlockables cannot be truly achieved and are selectively rewarded to specific individuals.

Humble Journey. Resource limitations can force administrators to focus solely on the elements, mechanics, and customization domains. However, this situation could lead to very labor- and time-intensive processes for administrators to deliver the programs or risk alienating a generation of students who expect the use of technology (Prensky, 2001). If any combination of domains would be deemed the weakest, it would likely be the humble journey, because it can create a completely customizable environment with robust content and assessment efforts and can integrate a high number of game-based elements without having the resources to make it easy to manage.

Opulent Gamification. This approach involves blending the elements and resources domains. Heavily integrating game elements with a resource-rich environment can create an exciting learning environment for students. Badges are an easy element of game design to incorporate into leadership competency development. For instance, each of the Student Leadership competencies (Seemiller, 2013) has its own digital badge that can be issued as students complete specific learning experiences aimed to enhance competency development, and institutions may develop their own based on their program offerings. Badging can be as simple as having one badge per competency where students must demonstrate learning to earn a badge. However, a more complex usage of badging would be to have one badge where the visual image of the badge is expanded as each activity is completed, resulting in the display of the full image of the final badge upon completion of all required achievements. In opulent gamification, a heavy emphasis would be placed on the design of these gamified elements, but there would not necessarily be a learning map to guide students through their experiences.

Wandering Expedition.   Programs focusing on the customization, resources, and elements domains may have a great infrastructure and delivery method to address leadership competencies, but by focusing too much on the customization domain, these programs may face challenges with participant attrition, long-term learning, and internalization of the competencies because students may be required to work too independently on competency development without being provided enough guidance and support. One particular component of motivation relies on a person's desire to interact with other people during their gamified experience (Yee, 2006). Whether it is a basic social interaction (virtual or in person) or the potential of developing long-term relationships with other people also engaged in the experience, individuals look for social connection. So, having a customized program that lacks a defined, cohort-based experience could result in students feeling isolated in their leadership learning. In addition, although achievement of competencies is an individual endeavor, some competencies, like those connected to group dynamics, relate more to interpersonal interactions or organizational behavior. By participating in leadership development with the same cohort throughout a program, a deeper level of interpersonal competency development might be achieved because of the level of familiarity and trust with these individuals.

Systematically Gamified.   This type of program brings together mechanics, resources, and elements, appearing as an opulent gamification program with the addition of mechanics. This allows for a guided and structured journey through the learning experience. Often professional staff sizes do not grow at the same rates as participation numbers, so customization is often one of the easiest domains to intentionally de-emphasize. This choice results in a program that aims to provide the most robust opportunity for the widest range of students with little to no room for students placing a personal stamp on their experience. For instance, a program may have bronze, silver, or gold levels of leadership requiring more time and energy as the student progresses through the levels. However, a student would not have a choice of what programs, workshops, or courses are included in these levels. Progression should, however, equate to deeper levels of learning. To connect levels to theory better, Seemiller (2013) references four specific dimensions—knowledge, value, ability, and behavior—that can act as built-in levels for each competency. The program could be set up to identify full completion of a competency by leveling up through all four dimensions. There may be additional achievement levels for students who complete all competencies related to their program of study or all within a specific category.

Conclusion

This chapter introduced the concepts of gamification and presented a new framework to integrate gamification into leadership competency development. The more comfortable educators are with the basic concepts of gamification, the more equipped they will be to apply them to leadership development experiences to engage today's college student. Although there are many ways to design student leadership programs to address competency development, intentionally planning experiences around the four domains of the gamification model can add a layer of sophistication to the program and can capitalize on students' motivations to succeed and persist in leadership education.

References

Cranford, R. (2016, July 25). "Pokemon Go" and social marketing. Arkansas Business. Retrieved from http://www.arkansasbusiness.com/article/112167/pokemon-go-and-social-marketing-ross-cranford-expert-advice

Deci, E., & Ryan, R. (1985). Intrinsic motivation and self-determination in human behavior. New York, NY: Plenum.

Deci, E., & Ryan, R. (2000). The "what" and "why" of goal pursuits: Human needs and the self-determination of behavior. Psychological Inquiry, 11, 227–268.

Deci, E., & Ryan, R. (2004). Handbook for self-determination research. Rochester, NY: University of Rochester Press.

Deterding, S. (2011). Situated motivational affordances of game elements: A conceptual model. Presented at CHI, 2011, Vancouver, BC, Canada. Retrieved from http://gamification-research.org/wp-content/uploads/2011/04/09-Deterding.pdf

Deterding, S., Sicart, M., Nacke, L., O'Hara, K., & Dixon, D. (2011). Gamification: Using game design elements in non-gaming contexts. Paper presented at CHI 2011, Vancouver, BC, Canada. Retrieved from http://gamification-research .org/wp-content/uploads/2011/04/01-Deterding-Sicart-Nacke-OHara-Dixon.pdf

Fitz-Walter, Z., Tjondronegoro, D., & Wyeth, P. (2011). Orientation passport: Using gamification to engage university students. In Proceedings of the 23rd Australian Computer–Human Interaction Conference, ACM, Australian National University, Canberra, ACT.

Haber, P. (2011). Formal leadership program models. In S. R. Komives, J. E. Owen, Slack, C., & Wagner, W. (Eds.), The handbook for student leadership development (pp. 231–258). San Francisco, CA: Jossey-Bass.

Hamari, J., Koivisto, J., & Sarsa, H. (2014). Does gamification work?—A literature review of empirical studies on gamification. Paper presented at the 47th Hawaii International Conference on Systems Science, Waikoloa, HI. Retrieved from http://people.uta.fi/~kljuham/2014-hamari_et_al-does_gamification_work.pdf

Isaacs, S. (2015, January 15). The difference between gamification and game-based learning [Web log post]. Retrieved from http://inservice.ascd.org/the-difference-between-gamification-and-game-based-learning/

Kotter, J. P. (1996). *Leading change*. Boston, MA: Harvard Business School Press.

Mekler, E., Brühlmann, F., Opwis, K., & Tuch, A. (2013). Do points, levels and leader-boards harm intrinsic motivation?: An empirical analysis of common gamification elements (pp. 66–73). In *Proceedings of the First International Conference on Gameful Design, Research, and Applications*, New York, NY.

Nicholson, S. (2012). A user-centered theoretical framework for meaningful gamification. *Games+ Learning+ Society, 8*, 223–230.

Prensky, M. (2001). Digital natives, digital immigrants. *On the Horizon, 9*(5), 1–5.

Raths, D. (2013, June 20). How badges really work in higher education. *Campus Technology*. Retrieved from https://campustechnology.com/articles/2013/06/20/how-badges-really-work-in-higher-education.aspx

Raths, D. (2015, August 19). Achieving student success through gamification. *Campus Technology*. Retrieved from http://campustechnology.com/articles/2015/08/19/achieving-student-success-through-non-academic-means.aspx.

Rose, D., & Meyer, A. (2002). *Teaching every student in the digital age: Universal design for learning*. Alexandria, VA: ASCD.

Seemiller, C. (2013). *The student leadership competencies guidebook: Designing intentional leadership learning and development*. San Francisco, CA: Jossey-Bass.

Yee, N. (2006). Motivations for play in online games. *CyberPsychology & Behavior, 9*, 772–775.

Adam R. Cebulski is the director of assessment and strategic initiatives at Southern Methodist University and is an independent consultant focusing on strategic planning, assessment, and change management within student affairs.

7

This chapter focuses on common pitfalls in assessing leadership competencies, simple strategies to avoid them, and innovative theoretical approaches and strategies in assessment.

Strategies in Assessment of Leadership Competencies

David M. Rosch, Kerry L. Priest

Riley is a student affairs advisor with a part-time teaching appointment at her university. She is responsible for coordinating LEAD 101, a 1-credit Emerging Leaders course held in the spring semester. The course is designed for first-year students who have been identified in student organizations across campus as having strong potential for future success. Having served in the role for the past several years, Riley feels the course has had a positive impact on many students. However, other than her teaching evaluations—which are focused more on students' satisfaction with their experience than on achieving course outcomes—she has little evidence to support her perspective. Moreover, although students repeatedly state that they find the course beneficial, some of them struggle to identify specific and concrete ways in which they have grown as a result of the experience.

Situations like Riley's are quite common. Recently, the Inter-Association Leadership Education Collaborative (ILEC) identified evidence-based practice through assessment and evaluation as a critical priority for leadership educators (Inter-Association Leadership Education Collaborative, 2016). The pressure to assess student leadership development accurately is driven by the need for effective leadership in educational, organizational, and community contexts. For example, in a study by the National Association of College and Employers (2016), 169 employers of university graduates list leadership and the ability to work in a team as more important than technical skills for success in the jobs for which they hire. In response to these pressures, and as a means to recruit, postsecondary institutions have invested heavily in curricular and co-curricular leadership development initiatives. The International Leadership Association lists nearly 2,000 formal academic leadership programs in higher education globally (International Leadership Association, 2015);

New Directions for Student Leadership, no. 156, Winter 2017 © 2017 Wiley Periodicals, Inc., A Wiley Company
Published online in Wiley Online Library (wileyonlinelibrary.com) • DOI: 10.1002/yd.20273

a number that is almost double what it was only a decade earlier (Riggio, Ciulla, & Sorensen, 2003). In conjunction, public corporations spend more than $60 billion annually through investments in the leadership development of their employees (Zenger, 2012).

Such significant and relatively recent focus on the leadership development of students and emerging adults has not necessarily resulted in consistent success or convincing data that show measurable growth in their leadership competencies. A recent national study revealed that although structured leadership education initiatives are generally correlated with increased leadership capacity of students who report participating in them, there is wide variation from program to program (Dugan et al., 2011). Such variation may not be surprising given the durable and vexing issues in assessing the leadership capacity of students (Rosch & Schwartz, 2009). As Roberts and Bailey (2016) suggest, "Leadership educators may have programs they think do an excellent job of preparing students . . . , but anecdotal evidence of this is no longer sufficient" (p. 8).

How do we know that students are developing leadership competencies? And how can we be sure if the significant time and money invested in leadership development initiatives are making a difference? This chapter will focus on such assessment issues, providing both an overview of assessment practices common in measuring the leadership competencies of students and a number of innovative ideas and suggestions for assessing leadership competencies. Riley will serve as a case example to help bring principles and strategies of assessment to life.

Strategic Considerations in Assessing Leadership Programs

Leadership assessment, at its foundation, is an organized process of collecting, making meaning of, and using data about what students know, understand, and can do with leadership-specific knowledge, often as the result of a developmental intervention (e.g., course, training, or experience). How do educators navigate this process in an intentional, systematic, and comprehensive way? Figure 7.1 illustrates four interrelated considerations for framing assessment efforts, answering the questions: Who? Why? What? How? It can be helpful to think of these four considerations like compass points on the assessment journey. They serve as a way of orienting oneself to the assessment process.

For example, Riley might teach a session in her Emerging Leaders course focused on the five "Thomas-Kilmann" methods of conflict management: avoiding, accommodating, compromising, competing, and collaborating (Thomas, 1992). This framework can help guide how Riley may approach assessing the leadership competency of conflict management.

Level (Who?). Assessment of leadership competencies happens across multiple domains, or levels of analysis (Owen, 2011). At the individual level, assessment serves to provide self-data to individuals for the

Figure 7.1.   Considerations of Leadership Assessment

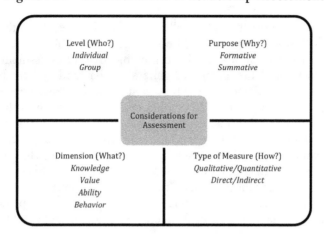

purpose of learning or improved performance. For example, Riley may incorporate a conflict management self-assessment into the leadership course as a way for individuals to identify self-information about their preferred style or approach to conflict. At the group level (e.g., classroom, team, or program level), the purpose of assessment is to provide data on the efficacy of interventions in impacting individual and/or collective learning (e.g., change in knowledge, beliefs, or skill). For example, Riley may also use a pre–post or post-only assessment in order to understand how much students learned, their confidence in their own conflict management skills, or frequency of engagement in conflict management activity. This group-level data can be valuable to instructors or facilitators as they reflect on their own teaching practice and utilize information gathered to make curricular improvements.

Purpose (Why?).   The previous examples also point to the various purposes of assessment. Formative assessments are improvement focused, designed to improve the quality of student learning by helping students identify their strengths and weaknesses or target areas that need development (Garrett & Camper, 2015; Sambell, McDowell, & Montgomery, 2012). They also provide feedback to facilitators or instructors that can inform ongoing instructional design and learning support (see also Angelo & Cross, 1993 for examples of formative classroom assessment techniques). The purpose of summative assessment is to evaluate student learning at the end of a program or instructional unit—usually against a benchmark or standard—with an emphasis on not only performance but also the understanding and capability that supports performance (Sambell et al., 2012). For example, Riley may give a final comprehensive exam to evaluate attainment of knowledge about conflict management. She may also utilize a conflict scenario and in-class demonstration to observe and assess students' use of conflict management behaviors directly.

Dimension (What?).   Seemiller (2013) identifies four dimensions within leadership competencies: knowledge, value, ability, and behavior. These dimensions can be considered the objectives of assessment. Knowledge refers to students' degree of general understanding of a particular competency and is demonstrated by recalling facts or basic concepts (e.g., What are the five approaches to conflict management?). The Value dimension refers to the value placed on the competency (e.g., How important is conflict management for leadership?). Ability describes students' capacity (motivation or skill) to engage in the behavior (e.g., How motivated are you to engage in conflict management? How confident are you in your ability to manage conflict?). Finally, the Behavior dimension looks at the actual engagement in a certain behavior associated with the competency (e.g., How frequently have you utilized effective conflict management in the past month?).

Types of Measure (How?).   Assessment data can be collected through multiple methods. Quantitative methods of data collection are in numerical form (e.g., multiple choice or rating scales), while qualitative methods primarily involve words or textual forms of data often derived from open-ended questions or narratives (Fraenkel & Wallen, 2006; Seemiller, 2016). Assessment methods can also be classified as direct or indirect. Direct measures of learning require a demonstration of knowledge and skills, including objective tests or observable performance measures such as essays, project presentations, or portfolios of accumulated work over time (Banta & Palomba, 2015). Indirect measures are representations of one's perception of learning or development through self-reported survey instruments, reflections on learning (e.g., essays or artistic expression), or exit surveys or interviews (Banta & Palomba, 2015). There are a number of resources that provide examples of competency-based rubric or checklists for self-assessment that can be utilized as indirect measures (e.g., Komives, Wagner, & Associates, 2017; Seemiller, 2016; 2016; Sessa, 2017).

A challenge with qualitative measurements is that analysis of the results can be subjective, and without a plan for analysis, one could spend a lot of time looking at results but not eliciting much meaning from the data. At the same time, quantitative measurements may lack nuance to understand the development process fully. Ideally, comprehensive assessment strategies (a leadership assessment plan) should incorporate qualitative and quantitative, as well as direct and indirect measures.

In Riley's case, giving a multiple-choice exam on the concepts of conflict management is an example of a quantitative, direct measure. Asking students to take a conflict-style inventory is a quantitative, indirect measure. Writing a self-reflection on a personal experience with conflict is a qualitative, indirect measure, whereas reviewing observer notes about a student's ability to engage in conflict management effectively would be a qualitative, direct measure.

Common Issues in Assessing Leadership Competencies

The strategic considerations of "who, what, when, and where" are only a starting point in creating an assessment plan. When planning for any journey, it is important to anticipate challenges. Similarly, leadership educators need to be aware of the problematic issues that can affect assessment efforts. Rosch and Schwartz (2009) summarized these issues by describing five negative effects associated with measuring change in student leadership-related educational outcomes.

The "Honeymoon Effect." The Honeymoon Effect is specific to the employment of a quantitative or qualitative assessment of leadership competencies immediately following participation in a leadership education intervention. Here, participants often overstate the level of their competence gained from the program, due in part to an often-unconscious desire to justify the time they invested in the program and their presumed ability to gain a targeted skill. In addition, posttest assessments can be helpful as a program evaluation tool if used longitudinally, where program iterations can be compared to each other, and therefore where the Honeymoon Effect can be accounted. However, the largest weakness of posttest assessments is that they are conducted without participants' ability to practice their competencies outside the context of a controlled environment, thus limiting the generalizability of the collected data.

The "Horizon Effect." In an attempt to control for posttest-only bias, leadership educators have employed pretests for participants to complete prior to an intervention. This method typically uses the same self-report instrument to collect data before and after a course or training intervention, as a way to assess change in knowledge or skill. However, this assessment design introduces a Horizon Effect (Rosch & Schwartz, 2009) more commonly known as response shift bias (Rohs, 2002) when conducted using quantitative assessments. This effect occurs when participants shift their perspectives regarding the accurate assessment of their competence as they learn more regarding the appropriate structure and depth of leadership competencies. For example, a participant may overestimate their capacity for multicultural leadership behavior prior to learning how complex the practice of such behavior is. The shift in one's perspective leaves the data collected during a pretest (and therefore any comparison made to it) as less valid.

The "Hollywood Effect." Perhaps the most widely encountered weakness in accurately assessing leadership competencies is what Rosch and Schwartz (2009) describe as the Hollywood Effect, where individuals are more inclined to rate themselves positively on attributes that are considered socially valuable, such as the effective practice of leadership. Given this effect, individuals who complete assessments of leadership competencies are likely to overestimate their own capacities relative to their peers, and thus rate themselves more highly than a knowledgeable observer might.

The "Halo Effect." In part to account for the Hollywood Effect, assessment administrators have introduced multirater feedback mechanisms into their assessment design. Here, observers of the individual being assessed rate that person's leadership competencies. Within professional settings, organizations have designed multirater assessment tools, described above. Although some believe observer data possess more validity than self-reported data (Atkins & Wood, 2002), Rosch and Schwartz (2009) identify a version of the Halo Effect (Thorndike, 1920) in observer-reported leadership competence assessments. A Halo Effect occurs when observers who possess a positive impression of an individual are then more likely to rate that individual positively in other unrelated areas. Within a leadership context, it has come to signify that observers' ratings of an individual with a variety of leadership competencies are often anchored around how those observers rate the individual in an area in which they know that person well. For example, if a supervisor believes an employee is highly effective at meeting project deadlines, the supervisor may be more likely to rate that employee as effective in another competency, such as managing conflict among the employee's subordinates—an area in which the supervisor may be less likely to have accurate information.

The "Hallmark Effect." Finally, Rosch and Schwartz (2009) identify the Hallmark Effect, which they describe as a bias inherent within an individual's rating of their leadership competencies due to their pre-existing beliefs regarding the societal practice of leadership. For example, past research (Arminio et al., 2000) reveals that underrepresented minorities on university campuses may, in part, equate the practice of leadership as "acting White." Presumably, the possession of these hallmarks for leading would depress an individual's quantitative and qualitative assessments of his or her leadership competencies.

Essential Assessment Tools

Even given the issues described above, leadership educators possess a number of tools that, when applied in combination, can provide a road map for rigorous assessment of leadership competency development. First, three popular types of leadership competency assessments, pre–post tests, multirater evaluations, and postprogram feedback, are described, and then some examples to help Riley (and others) implement these strategies within their own interventions are provided.

Pre–Post Assessments. Perhaps the most common strategy of assessing leadership competency development is the pre–post test, which despite some of the cautions presented earlier can still be a useful form of assessment. For example, in Riley's Emerging Leaders course, she might use a pretest and corresponding posttest as a direct measure of knowledge gained (through knowledge-based questions), or an indirect measure of change in self-perceived leadership efficacy (through a Likert-based rating scale). Pre–post assessments do not have to be quantitative. Riley may also use a qualitative pre–post design as an indirect measure of leadership competency. Students may complete a "what would you do" scenario prompt on the first day of class. Riley collects and reviews the responses, which provide insight into students starting point. She holds onto the written reflections until the end of the semester. Then, the same scenario and prompt are given at the end of the course. Students then receive both of their responses and are asked to reflect on the changes they observe in their own responses, allowing for deeper levels of learning. Then, the reflections are collected and rated by the instructor on change in evidence of knowledge, values, and ability related to course concepts. Although this is not a direct measure of behavioral change, the qualitative pre–post design provides instructors the ability to see a more complete picture of not only what conceptual knowledge students possess, but also their increasing capacity to put their knowledge into practice.

Multirater Evaluations.   Multirater evaluations are a method of systematically collecting feedback about an individual's performance from a wide range of sources, including peers, teammates, direct reports, supervisors, advisors, instructors, or customers (Chappelow, 2004). Usually, this form of assessment includes a report that allows an individual to compare self-reported scores to others' feedback to offer a more complete picture of their current capacity, areas of development, and insight into how others see them. For example, students completing an internship might ask for ratings of performance from co-workers and employers as part of an evaluative portfolio. In the case of Riley's Emerging Leaders course, her students could use a multirater process to assess the competency of Verbal Communication at the individual behavioral level, as well as the group-level measure. She can set up a midpoint and a final checkpoint for students to rate each other and offer feedback on their communication behaviors. Additionally, she can provide an observed rating of the team's performance. Both sets of feedback might be integrated into each student's final reflection paper.

Postprogram Reflections.   Postprogram reflection assignments are also commonly used as a form of assessment. These qualitative or quantitative measures usually have specific prompts designed to assess learning and application to specific leadership-oriented objectives. For example, students enrolled in the Emerging Leaders course might be asked to write a detailed response to prompts such as, "Please describe in a concrete and specific way how your knowledge of successful leadership behaviors has increased as a result of completing this Emerging Leaders course." The use of a detailed rubric can be helpful for assessing student growth. In this instance, Riley might be interested in counting the number of concepts or competencies the student identifies, assessing if these concepts are accurately described and if specific behaviors unique to the student are pinpointed.

A challenge for leadership educators in an academic course like Riley's is that the grades students earn within this type of assignment are not necessarily directly reflective of student development or learning, but rather a representation of how the student response did or did not demonstrate key learning objectives. Still, the assessment data can be useful for educators in making informed decisions regarding the degree of impact their program or course possesses.

Innovative Theoretical Approaches to Assessment

Now oriented to the language and landscape of assessment and having identified some basic tools, theoretical considerations around assessment of leadership competencies can be addressed. Most educators are operating from theories of leadership, learning, and development, whether formal or informal, that guide their curricular and pedagogical choices. In this section, five theoretical approaches to competency development will be discussed. Employing one or more of these approaches indicate the values educators place on the type of development they are interested in assessing. This section will highlight cognitive, behavioral, constructivist, orthogenetic, and eudaimonic models while unpacking their assumptions and offering definitions of development and examples of assessment within each. Each has its own strengths and areas of focus, and skilled assessors of leadership competencies should incorporate aspects from several of these approaches to create a comprehensive and inclusive structure for the assessment efforts.

Cognitive Approach.   A cognitive approach to leadership development focuses on an individual's knowledge of who a leader is and what leadership entails, as well as mental processes (sense-making) Day, Harrison, & Halpin, 2009). Bloom's (1956) taxonomy of educational objectives (and later revisions, e.g., Krathwohl, 2002) offer a hierarchy of knowledge from lower order (e.g., remembering, understanding, and applying) to higher order (e.g., analyzing, evaluating, and creating). At a basic level, cognitive assessment of leadership competencies emphasizes identifying and describing the theories and concepts of leadership, as well as behaviors, thoughts, or emotions that result in leadership success. In Riley's case, knowledge can be very simple to assess, for example, by asking students to list and describe the various theories covered in her course. As a way of assessing higher-order cognition, Riley may use a case study scenario that requires students to apply, analyze, and evaluate concepts in a specific context. Or, students may select a theory or concept and conduct an original research project to advance that topic.

Behavioral Approach.   Behavioral approaches emphasize enacted behavior rather than knowledge. Behavioral theories of leadership may suggest that individuals have preferences for behaviors, but that behaviors can be developed and adapted to suit the needs of a situation. Thus, a behavioral assessment seeks to identify strengths, weaknesses, or preferences of behaviors for the purpose of self-information, as well as to identify areas of development. Most self-report and multirater style assessments focus on this model, with an emphasis on outward expression of actions and results.

For example, the Leadership Practices Inventory (LPI) Kouzes & Posner, 2003) utilizes both self-assessment and multirater assessment to evaluate how frequently one engages in a set of leadership behaviors and how frequently others perceive them enacting those behaviors. A key assumption behind assessments like the LPI is the belief that students who utilize the behaviors identified within the assessment more frequently will be more effective as a leader. In Riley's case, she may wish to use the Thomas-Kilmann Indicator (TKI), which is a behavioral assessment of conflict-handling modes, or ways of dealing with conflict (Schaubhut, 2007). Although behavioral assessment is relatively simple to assess, a central weakness of many behavioral assessments is that the context in which those behaviors are used and/or cultural factors that may impact a leader's or group member's perceptions is commonly not considered.

Constructivist Approach.   This approach is grounded in constructivist theory, which states that people come to their own understanding of the world and make meaning of it through the prism of their own perspectives and experiences (Robinson, 2012). At its base, a constructivist approach to assessing leadership competency development incorporates invitations for students to engage in active learning and experimentation in implementing a particular competency, and then to critically reflect on their experience to inform their future actions. A common form of constructivist assessment is the reflection paper—where educators invite students to reflect in critical and organized ways to inform their own leadership behaviors and goals for learning. Over the course of repeated efforts, students begin to develop deep and significant meaning regarding how they will practice leading and leadership in the context of their own lives.

Applying a strategic constructivist-based assessment approach might involve placing students in a position to learn and then reflect on their application of material in personally meaningful ways so that learning can be productively applied in the unique context of each student. For example, after first being exposed to the five methods of conflict management discussed earlier, Riley might ask students to identify which method (or methods) they individually prefer to apply in most situations. After repeated exposure to various cases or actual scenarios, as well as practice in applying each method, she might ask students to reflect critically on their own personal style in applying each of the five methods and identify specific behaviors in which they feel they need additional practice. In using a constructivist approach, therefore, leadership educators are able to measure and evaluate specific and unique ways each student makes meaning of and applies specific leadership-related constructs.

Orthogenetic Approach.   Somewhat related to a constructivist approach is one that employs orthogenetic aspects to competency assessment practices. Orthogenetic development originated from a biological sciences foundation, referring to cells differentiating from other cells, articulating unique purposes, and becoming integrated with other cells to form more complex organisms (Werner, 1940). In social sciences, orthogenetic human development refers to change within someone that brings about higher levels of personal complexity in understanding oneself and how one interacts with the world (Robinson, 2012). Orthogenetic development can be assessed by determining the complexity of students' understanding and personal application of concepts, as well as their ability to integrate their understanding of other factors that affect intent, such as the environment.

The field of leadership development is ripe with concepts that may seem cognitively simple on the surface but possess significant complexity and interrelatedness with other concepts when applied in practice. For example, many leadership programs include curriculum designed to augment participants' "communication skills." A minimum understanding might be represented in students who can describe their communication style in broad terms. A more developed understanding might come with the ability to recognize when their styles shift with their mood or goals of the conversation. An even more developed perspective might be displayed in students who recognize how their personal histories and current environment might affect their communication behaviors. As with constructivist assessment, orthogenetic assessment is most effective when it is qualitative in structure and attends to the degree to which students possess complex and integrated ideas of their leadership competencies.

Eudaimonic Approach.   Eudaimonic development represents, at its essence, a growing sense of fulfillment and well-being in one's life (Robinson, 2012). In this sense, well-being is more than personal happiness and also includes the possession of purpose in one's life, self-acceptance, and positive relationships with others in one's environment. Within the framework of leadership learning and development, a eudaimonic focus might include helping students develop a personal sense of how their leadership-specific goals are related to helping them achieve their broader life goals, how students might evolve a sense of self that includes taking on leadership roles in various environments, how to develop authentic and personally fulfilling relationships with team members that help them grow as people as much as achieve team goals, or how to inculcate a sense of curiosity and desire to continue learning about leadership long after the conclusion of one's formal education. Following these general priorities, a eudaimonic approach to the assessment of leadership competencies might invite students to report the degree to which they feel a sense of their

NEW DIRECTIONS FOR STUDENT LEADERSHIP • DOI: 10.1002/yd

Table 7.1 Leadership Assessment Planning Questions

Context	Questions
Who	Who am I assessing—an individual, a group, or both?
Why	What is the purpose of my assessment? To provide feedback for learning (formative) or evaluation (summative)?
	Why are these data important? What will I use these data for?
What	What competency do I plan to assess?
	What theoretical approach(es) am I taking in my assessment?
	On what dimension(s) (knowledge, value, ability, behavior) should data collection be focused?
How	How will I get the data? What tools will I use (instruments, forms, etc.)?
	What type(s) of measurements will I use? Qualitative, quantitative, direct, and/or indirect?
	How can I mitigate any potential issues or drawbacks in my assessment method or with the instrument I will be using?
Now what?	What do these data mean for my course or program? How will I respond to these results?

purpose in life as a leader, or the extent to which the practice of a particular leadership competency helps them to achieve their personal goals.

Conclusion

There is no one-size-fits-all approach to assessment; one's efforts should be as unique as one's intended outcomes. Still, it is essential for leadership educators like Riley to consider how to incorporate meaningful assessment at a variety of levels that incorporate multiple dimensions in pursuit of evidence-based practice that supports meaningful leader development. Table 7.1 offers a set of reflective planning questions for educators to consider when planning their assessment initiatives. This chapter has offered common issues in leadership competency assessment, as well as key considerations for effectively employing strategies that lead to intentional, systematic, comprehensive assessment of leadership competencies.

References

Angelo, T. A., & Cross, K. P. (1993). *Classroom assessment techniques: A handbook for college teachers* (2nd ed.). San Francisco, CA: Jossey-Bass.

Arminio, J. L., Carter, S., Jones, S. E., Kruger, K., Lucas, N., Washington, J., ... Scott, A. (2000). Leadership experiences of students of color. *NASPA Journal, 37*, 496–510.

Atkins, P. W. B., & Wood, R. E. (2002). Self- versus others ratings as predicators of assessment center ratings: Validation evidence for 360-degree feedback programs. *Personnel Psychology, 55*, 871–904.

Banta, T. W., & Palomba, C. A. (2015). *Assessment essentials: Planning, implementing, and improving assessment in higher education* (2nd ed.). San Francisco, CA: Jossey-Bass.

Bloom, B. S. (1956). *Taxonomy of educational objectives, handbook I: The cognitive domain.* New York, NY: David McKay Co Inc.

Chappelow, C. T. (2004). 360-degree feedback. In C. D. McCauley & E. V. Velsor (Eds.), *Center for creative leadership handbook of leadership development* (2nd ed., pp. 58–84). San Francisco, CA: Jossey-Bass.

Day, D. V., Harrison, M. M., & Halpin, S. (2009). *An integrative approach to leader development: Connecting adult development, identity, and expertise.* New York, NY: Routledge.

Dugan, J. P., Bohle, C. W., Gebhardt, M., Hofert, M., Wilk, E., & Cooney, M. (2011). Influences of leadership program participation on students' capacities for socially responsible leadership. *Journal of Student Affairs Research and Practice, 48,* 65–84. https://doi.org/10.2202/1949-6605.6206.

Fraenkel, J. R., & Wallen, N. E. (2006). *How to design and evaluate research in education* (6th ed.). New York, NY: McGraw-Hill.

Garrett, J. M., & Camper, J. M. (2015). Formative assessment as an effective leadership learning tool. *New Directions for Student Leadership, 145,* 97–106.

Inter-Association Leadership Education Collaborative. (2016). *Collaborative priorities and critical considerations for leadership education.* Retrieved from https://nclp.umd.edu

International Leadership Association. (2015). *Leadership program directory.* Retrieved from http://www.ila-net.org/Resources/LPD/index.htm.

Komives, S. R., Wagner, W., & Associates. (2017). *Leadership for a better world: Understanding the social change model of leadership development* (2nd ed.). San Francisco, CA: Jossey-Bass.

Kouzes, J. M., & Posner, B. Z. (2003). *The Leadership Practices Inventory (LPI): Participant's workbook.* New York, NY: John Wiley & Sons.

Krathwohl, D. R. (2002). A revision of Bloom's taxonomy: An overview. *Theory Into Practice, 41,* 212–218.

National Association of Colleges and Employers. (2016). *The attributes employers seek on a candidate's resume.* Retrieved from http//www.naceweb.org/talent-acquisition/candidate-selection/the-attributes-employers-seek-on-a-candidates-resume/

Owen, J. E. (2011). Assessment and evaluation. In S. R. Komives, J. P. Dugan, J. E. Owen, C. Slack, & W. Wagner (Eds.), *The handbook for student leadership development* (2nd ed.). San Francisco, CA: Jossey-Bass.

Riggio, R. E., Ciulla, J. B., & Sorensen, G. J. (2003). Leadership education at the undergraduate level: A liberal arts approach to leadership development. In S. E. Murphy & R. E. Riggio (Eds.), *The future of leadership development* (pp. 223–236). Mahwah, NJ: Erlbaum.

Roberts, D. M., & Bailey, K. J. (Eds.). (2016). *New Directions in Student Leadership, 151.*

Robinson, O. (2012). *Development through adulthood: An integrative sourcebook.* New York, NY: Palgrave Macmillan.

Rohs, F. R. (2002). Improving the evaluation of leadership programs: Control response-shift bias. *Journal of Leadership Education, 1*(2), 50–61.

Rosch, D. M., & Schwartz, L. M. (2009). Potential issues and pitfalls in outcomes assessment in leadership education. *Journal of Leadership Education, 8,* 177–194.

Sambell, K., McDowell, L., & Montgomery, C. (2012). *Assessment for learning in higher education.* New York, NY: Routledge.

Schaubhut, N. A. (2007). *Technical brief for the Thomas-Kilmann Conflict Mode Instrument: Description of the updated normative sample and implications for use.* Retrieved from: https://www.cpp-qa.com/Pdfs/TKI_Technical_Brief.pdf

Seemiller, C. (2013). *The student leadership competencies guidebook: Developing intentional leadership learning and development.* San Francisco, CA: Jossey-Bass.

Seemiller, C. (2016). *Student leadership competencies implementation handbook*. Retrieved from www.studentleadershipcompetencies.com

Sessa, V. I. (2017). *College student leadership development*. New York: Routledge.

Thomas, K. W. (1992). Conflict and conflict management: Reflections and update. *Journal of Organizational Behavior, 13*, 265–274.

Thorndike, E. L. (1920). A constant error in psychological ratings. *Journal of Applied Psychology, 4*, 25–29.

Werner, H. (1940). *Comparative psychology of mental development*. New York, NY: International Universities Press, Inc.

Zenger, J. (2012, May 2). Does leadership development really work? *Forbes*. Retrieved from http://www.forbes.com/sites/jackzenger/2012/05/02/does-leadership-development-really-work-2/

DAVID M. ROSCH *serves as an associate professor at the University of Illinois at Urbana-Champaign, where his research and teaching is focused on the leadership development of young people.*

KERRY L. PRIEST *is an assistant professor in the Staley School of Leadership Studies at Kansas State University. Her scholarship explores the intersections of leadership development and engaged teaching and learning practices in higher education.*

8

This chapter outlines a process used by a large, public, research institution to create and implement a competency-based leadership development initiative across campus.

Building a Competency-Based Leadership Program with Campus-Wide Implementation

Kelley C. Ashby, Paul J. Mintner

In the fall of 2014, members of the University of Iowa's Student Success Team came together to discuss strategies that would attract more in-state students to attend the institution. One suggestion that arose from this gathering was to enhance leadership development efforts campus-wide. This chapter describes the process of creating a campus-wide leadership initiative from idea exploration to implementation.

The Context

The University of Iowa's Student Success Team (SST) began in 2006 and includes faculty and staff from every organization and college on campus (Student Life, Provost Office, Athletics, Libraries, Information Technology Services, International Programs, and all undergraduate and professional colleges). The purpose of the SST is to "develop ideas and implement initiatives that foster undergraduate achievement within a safe, engaging, and inclusive campus community" (The University of Iowa, n.d.). SST helps make "significant changes in the undergraduate student experience at Iowa" (Hansen, n.d.). There are 556 members on the SST listserv; 200 of those are actively involved in various SST initiatives. Oversight of SST is provided by the executive team: Vice President of Student Life, Associate Provost for Undergraduate Education, and Associate Vice President of Student Life.

Each fall, the Student Success Team has a retreat where ideas are discussed for the upcoming year (Hansen, n.d.). In the fall of 2014, the focus of the SST retreat was to generate ideas on how the university could maintain and enhance the undergraduate experience. SST members formed small

NEW DIRECTIONS FOR STUDENT LEADERSHIP, no. 156, Winter 2017 © 2017 Wiley Periodicals, Inc., A Wiley Company
Published online in Wiley Online Library (wileyonlinelibrary.com) • DOI: 10.1002/yd.20274

groups to discuss several ideas that might accomplish this that were shared with the larger group. Subsequently, each SST member voted for one best idea, and the ideas that received the most votes were passed along to the SST executive team to approve. One idea that made it through this process was to make the University of Iowa recognized as *the* Regents institution known for creating leaders.

Since 2009, senior administrators at the University of Iowa have had a desire to expand leadership experiences for undergraduate students. In addition to a change in the makeup of key staff members and administrators, fall 2014 appeared to be the ideal time for expanding leadership initiatives. This was because of changes in the state funding model, the push for higher education accountability, an emphasis on student employability, and the prominence of high-impact practices already offered across campus.

State Funding Model.   The primary factor that laid the groundwork for discussions on expanding leadership initiatives centered around a proposed change in how the Board of Regents, State of Iowa would fund institutions of higher education in the state. This shift would place greater emphasis on in-state student recruitment, requiring the University of Iowa to adapt its recruitment focus (Agnew, 2014). Faculty and staff were concerned about how the University of Iowa may meet this new expectation, which led to some discussion about the unique value propositions around leadership development that the University of Iowa could offer to recruit undergraduate students more heavily.

Higher Education Accountability.   In addition, faculty and staff at the University of Iowa were keenly aware of several shifting trends in higher education in general. National conversations about retention on college campuses as well as the need to showcase value as part of the Obama administration's college "accountability-push" (Supiano, 2015) provided additional rationale to faculty and staff to consider expanding leadership development opportunities for undergraduate students at the University of Iowa. Specifically, the need for accountability for workforce preparation (Kelderman, 2015) and the need to demonstrate the value of a degree (Berrett, 2016) were key areas that administrators hoped a pervasive leadership development initiative might address.

Employment Preparation.   In addition to the shifting trends and expectations for higher education, emphasis on employability and skepticism from employers about the role higher education plays in building qualities and skills necessary to be successful in the workplace (Fabris, 2015) provided additional evidence for strengthening the undergraduate leadership development experience. University of Iowa's faculty and staff looked to the National Association of Colleges and Employers (2016) for guidance as to what employers were looking for in new hires to help understand how institutional goals of leadership development for undergraduate students could meet employers' needs.

High-Impact Practices.   Finally, as faculty and staff contemplated expanding leadership experiences for undergraduates, it was determined that the university already had many leadership development experiences for undergraduate students offered in various departments, many of which were high-impact practices. Kuh (2008) asserts that high-impact practices "typically demand that students devote considerable time and effort to purposeful tasks" (p. 14), allowing them to transfer learning across contexts and receive frequent feedback on their learning. These opportunities were plentiful, and many students were already taking advantage of educationally purposeful activities related to leadership. However, like many college campuses, the "utilization of active learning practices [had been] unsystematic" (p. 9) on campus, with most high-impact practices happening in isolation of one another. It was not likely that students were connecting their learning from experience to experience. Without providing an intentional way for these connections to occur, students may struggle with articulating learning, building upon leadership development experiences, and perhaps most importantly, effectively articulating competencies gained in their time at the University of Iowa with potential employers or as they applied to graduate school.

Idea Exploration

Shortly after the fall 2014 Student Success Team retreat, a charge was given to develop this "leadership experience idea" into a proposal that would be submitted to the SST executive team. Two staff members who worked primarily with leadership development were asked to co-chair a small team of faculty and staff from across campus that would write this proposal, focusing on how to provide every undergraduate student with a leadership experience. The overarching goal was for the institution to be recognized as *the* University that creates leaders who leverage their strengths, leadership knowledge, and leadership skills to contribute to their communities now and in the future.

From Idea to Proposal

It was important to ensure that the members of the team who would write the proposal came from a wide variety of departments and represented both entry-level and mid-manager roles to make sure the voices of those working most closely with students and those who had decision-making authority were included. The proposal development team included 11 people overall (including the co-chairs) and consisted of representatives from Orientation, Residence Life and Living–Learning Communities, Student Organizations and Co-Curricular Programs, Career Advising, Academic Advising, and Academic Courses. Each team member was asked to recruit others, who did similar work, to build a small advisory team and to bring ideas from their units about how they could contribute toward helping the University of Iowa become *the* Regents institution known for creating leaders. The team had 9 months to develop a proposal.

The Leadership Development Approach.   For many years prior to fall 2014, leadership development opportunities for undergraduates were being offered but by various units across campus that were operating in silos. Offices lacked interest in working collaboratively, and each unit functioned without a unifying vision for leadership development. Despite the lack of organizational cohesiveness, there was administrative interest from the Vice President of Student Life and the Associate Provost for Undergraduate Education to develop a leadership initiative for University of Iowa students. Between 2012 and 2014, several conversations about becoming a "Strengths campus" through Gallup[1] had occurred, and a few proposals had been submitted to upper administration. These proposals never gained any traction for implementation, mainly because of lack of funding. However, as a part of designing a campus-wide leadership initiative, we were charged to revisit these ideas and include strengths development in the proposal. Several people believed that simply having students complete the Clifton Strengths-Finder assessment from Gallup was not providing them with a "leadership experience" and would not solely result in the University of Iowa being recognized as *the* University that creates leaders who leverage their strengths, leadership knowledge, and leadership skills to contribute to their communities now and in the future. According to Rath (2007), "scientists have discovered that core personality traits are relatively stable throughout adulthood, as are our passions and interests ... and StrengthsFinder measures the elements of your personality that are less likely to change—your talents" (p. 18). Rath, however, continues by saying, "The most successful people start with dominant talent—and then add skills, knowledge, and practice to the mix" (p. 19). It was clear that adding knowledge and skills components to understanding strengths could provide a comprehensive way to accomplish the overall goal of student leadership development (Komives, Lucas, & McMahon, 2013). The challenge was finding the right skills, knowledge, and practice pieces that would be applicable in both the academic and cocurricular arenas to complement the Clifton StrengthsFinder assessment.

After researching options, it appeared that the Student Leadership Competencies (Seemiller, 2013b) could be that piece. The Student Leadership Competencies reflect a skill-based approach, which "makes leadership available to everyone, because skills are competencies that people can learn or develop" (Northouse, 2015, p. 5). Thus, the focus could be on having all students understand their inherited talents (traits) and then increase their knowledge and skills (competencies) associated with those talents, so they could leverage their strengths, leadership knowledge, and leadership skills to prepare them for the future (work, graduate school, and community membership). Chapter 3 in this volume maps leadership competencies onto strengths.

Educating the Proposal Team to Gain Buy-In.   Not all members of the proposal development team were leadership experts. Educating the team on the two major components of the initiative was critical to gather ideas and secure commitment before writing the proposal. First, any team members who were not confident in their understanding of Gallup strengths (Rath, 2007) were asked to participate in the Human Resources Organizational Effectiveness department's training on strengths. Second, only a few team members (mainly those directly responsible for providing leadership development and education for students) had some knowledge of the Student Leadership Competencies (Seemiller, 2013b). The team solicited the assistance of the author of the *Student Leadership Competencies Guidebook* (Seemiller, 2013b) to educate our proposal development team, the subcommittees, and the Student Success Team about how the Student Leadership Competencies (Seemiller, 2013b) could be infused into the work of various departments across the institution. The author first met virtually with several subcommittees and then came to campus to educate the Student Success Team and to work directly with the subcommittees. This process was critical in helping to gain buy-in for the idea across campus.

Writing the Proposal.   Each member of the proposal development team was asked to submit a description and a timeline about how the Gallup strengths (Rath, 2007) and the Student Leadership Competencies (Seemiller, 2013b) could be infused into their services and programs along with a list of any financial or additional human resources needed for new programs or opportunities. The Executive Officers of the departments represented on the proposal development team were asked to submit a letter of support that would be included with the proposal. These letters outlined how the unit was already using and/or planned to use the Gallup strengths (Rath, 2007) and Student Leadership Competencies (Seemiller, 2013b) in their services and programs.

The co-chairs collected this information and wrote a proposal for the SST executive team to review. Shortly after, the SST executive team approved the majority of the strategies included in the proposal. No additional funding or human resources were designated to assist with implementing these strategies except for the funding to cover the costs of the Clifton Strengths-Finder assessments for all first-year and transfer students.

Gaining Buy-In.   Attention was given to gaining buy-in from the very beginning of the proposal development process and continued even into the implementation phase. In the beginning, it was critical to build a team of faculty and staff members to assist with the proposal development stage to begin gaining buy-in for the idea of what exactly would be needed to become *the* Regents institution that creates leaders. It was important to recognize the need to identify various roles the different units on campus might play to make this initiative successful. The roles are listed below.

- *Initiators* were those who would be the "first" to introduce students to the Gallup strengths (Rath, 2007) and Student Leadership Competencies (Seemiller, 2013b).
- *Referral Agents* were those who would discuss Gallup strengths (Rath, 2007) and Student Leadership Competencies (Seemiller, 2013b) with students to help them make academic and/or career development decisions as well as help guide them to classes and other opportunities where they could learn more about their strengths or to develop competencies.
- *Educators* were those who would be primarily responsible for developing classes, workshops, trainings, and other educational programs that intentionally focused on Gallup strengths (Rath, 2007) and Student Leadership Competencies (Seemiller, 2013b).
- *Coaches* were those who would serve as mentors and help reinforce Gallup strengths (Rath, 2007) and Student Leadership Competencies (Seemiller, 2013b) outside of a "formal" class, workshop, or training and use the two as tools to assist students in experiences such as leadership, athletics, or student employment.
- *General Supporters* were those who could make the most of a teachable moment by engaging students in conversations about Gallup strengths (Rath, 2007) and Student Leadership Competencies (Seemiller, 2013b).

Several faculty and staff, departments, and informal groups could serve in several of the roles at various points during their interactions with different students. For example, the staff members and student leaders responsible for orientation would play the role of "initiators" when introducing Gallup strengths (Rath, 2007) to incoming students, while orientation staff members would also serve as "educators" and "coaches" during their work preparing the orientation student leaders to engage incoming students with Gallup strengths (Rath, 2007).

From Proposal to Implementation

There were several significant components that were instrumental to the success of this initiative. These included institutional commitments, human resource time, and technological resources.

Institutional Commitment.   First, it is important to point out that decision makers like the Associate Provost for Undergraduate Education, Vice President for Student Life, and Associate Vice President for Student Life demonstrated public commitment by sharing campus-wide communication related to the initiative as well as providing public forums like the SST meetings to encourage both buy-in and offer updates related to this initiative.

Second, the proposal team secured and received letters of support from departments whose work would be affected by the initiative to ensure the leadership development experiences could be implemented and sustained.

New Directions for Student Leadership • DOI: 10.1002/yd

These letters yielded important commitments from the University College (including Orientation Services and New Student Initiatives), the Pomerantz Career Center, the Academic Advising Center, the Department of Residence Education, the College of Business Undergraduate Program Office, the College of Liberal Arts and Sciences, and the Center for Student Involvement and Leadership.

Human Resource Time.   The transition from proposal to implementation on campus necessitated a change in structure as well. The initial proposal team, made up of representatives from 10 departments, transitioned to a leaner implementation team with various domains of responsibility as outlined in Figure 8.1. Specific people were also appointed as leaders in supporting marketing and design needs, as well as work related to assessment.

Figure 8.1.   **Strengths and Student Leadership Competencies Implementation Team Structure**

Be Better @ Iowa Implementation Team				
Incentive Program	**Academic Trainers & Consultants**	**Resources Toolkit**	**Introductory Training**	**Train the Trainers**
1. Solicits high-impact experiences from departments that "count" for the incentive program 2. Markets incentive program 3. Tracks student completion of experiences in the incentive program	1. Determine Iowa's top SLCs 2. Train faculty 3. Assist faculty with mapping/infusing SLCs and Strengths into their syllabi and curriculum 4. Help recruit faculty/academic departments to engage in initiative	1. Develops curriculum, training, and resources on Iowa's top SLCs and Strengths for use with students 2. Develops assessment tools to measure impact	Develops and delivers training to staff that teaches them: 1. An overview of SLCs and Strengths 2. How to have conversations about SLCs and Strengths 3. Infusing SLCs and Strengths into working with students 4. Determines marketing pieces for those who complete training to display in their offices	Develops and delivers training for staff on: 1. How to train other staff and faculty 2. How to train peer leaders to use SLCs and Strengths in their work with other students 3. How to infuse SLCs and Strengths into work with student employees and interns 4. Develop weekly conversation starters that focus on SLCs and Strengths 5. Develop "quick tips" resources

NEW DIRECTIONS FOR STUDENT LEADERSHIP • DOI: 10.1002/yd

Most of the people on the implementation team were part of the proposal team, which offered the opportunity to build upon team members' knowledge of the initiative. A new team member joined based on his experience using the Student Leadership Competencies (Seemiller, 2013b) comprehensively in his department, and a marketing expert who had not been engaged in the initiative was invited to help refine the message to campus, create a communication plan, and develop materials to support the initiative. This group was also responsible for developing the name of the initiative: "Be Better @ Iowa." This name was selected because it reflected a goal of individual improvement as a student, employee, citizen, and leader. It also reflected the developmental process that all students were expected to experience through their time at the University of Iowa. It was important for the team that the Be Better @ Iowa initiative was not viewed as only a first-year student program, but rather as part of a student's entire experience at the university from orientation to commencement.

Also of note was the creation of an affinity group of departmental liaisons dedicated to furthering the goals of the initiative in individual departments. This group of liaisons would receive up-to-date information about the implementation team's progress and inform their departments of any pertinent updates to the "Be Better @ Iowa" initiative. Additionally, the leaders of the liaison group would act as both a sounding board for departmental needs and intermediaries to secure additional departmental commitments to utilize the Gallup strengths (Rath, 2007) and Student Leadership Competencies (Seemiller, 2013b) with students.

Technological Resources.   Finally, several important technological resources allowed the change process to be implemented across the institution. First, using online content management systems allowed the proposal and implementation teams to work efficiently in their own areas while contributing to the initiative as a whole. Additionally, the capability to communicate with the author remotely using Skype was invaluable to build understanding and institutional buy-in around the Student Leadership Competencies conceptual framework (Seemiller, 2013b). These specific technological resources are not to be understated, as they have helped a complex large research institution enact campus-wide change efficiently.

Key Strategies

Being strategic about how to break down a complex initiative into manageable (and realistic) pieces in order to maintain momentum has been invaluable.

Helpful or Necessary?   Along the way, the co-chairs continually had to determine the value of a task or idea by asking: "Is this *necessary* for this initiative to be successful?" or "Is this something that would be *helpful*, but not necessary, given human resource limitations?" Two examples of tasks that were scrutinized in this way were the development of a stakeholder communication plan and the selection of the university's top 11 competencies (out of the total 60).

Helpful: A Stakeholder Communication Plan.   Early in the process, it became clear that with appropriate human resources, it would have been beneficial to implement a stakeholder strategic communication plan. This plan would include identifying the key stakeholders associated with the "Be Better @ Iowa" initiative, their level of commitment (awareness, understanding, buy-in, or ownership), and the type and frequency of communication each should receive to keep them informed about the initiative's progress. Given the human resource limitations, the co-chairs were restricted with the amount of time each had to devote to advancing "Be Better @ Iowa" (both took on 25% additional work to lead this initiative on top of their current responsibilities). If the co-chairs had the time or more human resources, implementing a stakeholder plan would have easily been a "necessity." Instead, the co-chairs met monthly with the Associate Vice President for Student Life to keep her informed of the status of the initiative.

Necessary: Selecting Institutional Competencies.   Early on, the co-chairs were strongly encouraged by the author of the Student Leadership Competencies (Seemiller, 2013b) not to try to include all 60 of the competencies in the initiative. Instead, she suggested identifying approximately 10 to become the University of Iowa's top 10. To do this, a graduate student was assigned the task of compiling a list of every undergraduate major offered at the university and looking up each major in the Jossey-Bass Student Leadership Competencies Database (Seemiller, 2013a) to find the competencies associated with each major. The student then created a sortable spreadsheet that included all of this information. Once the spreadsheet was complete, it was easy to identify which competencies were listed most often. From there, the list was analyzed to ensure that it was inclusive of competencies essential in all undergraduate academic colleges. The goal was to have at least one competency from each undergraduate college on the "top 10 list," and this goal was ultimately achieved. Finally, the team took into consideration the university's mission and institutional values, the Iowa Challenge (the university's expectations of its students), the current campus climate reflected in the campus-wide goal of enhancing the University of Iowa's undergraduate experience, and the National Association of Colleges and Employers (2016) workforce competencies to further reduce the larger list down to University of Iowa's top 11 competencies. These competencies include Analysis, Problem Solving, Verbal Communication, Writing, Diversity, Productive Relationships, Collaboration, Self-Development, Ethics, Goals, and Group Development (Seemiller, 2013b).

Creation of New Programs Versus Alignment.   An important distinction related to the creation of "Be Better @ Iowa" was the desire to adapt or align already existing programs with Gallup strengths (Rath, 2007) and the Student Leadership Competencies (Seemiller, 2013b). In the cases where this was not possible, new programs were created.

Adapting.   It was clear that there was a need to adapt existing services to reflect how the competencies may be used. For instance, a monthly lunch and learn offered by the Center for Student Involvement and Leadership called the "Leadership Development Series," with various, yet haphazardly selected, topics covered throughout the year, was adjusted to include topics like "Using your Strengths for Collaboration" or "Using your Strengths for Problem Solving." Both of these sessions effectively bring together both concepts in the leadership initiative and promote a more defined understanding for students about the outcomes of their own investment in leadership development through attending each program.

Aligning.   In some cases, all that was necessary was to align specific competencies related to the goals of the work that departments were already doing with students, without having to adapt those programs. This meant experiences like resident assistant training would largely stay the same, but when appropriate, leadership competencies would be named and used to strengthen curriculum as well as students' understanding of the competencies they gain through the training.

Creating New Programs.   Though much of the work involved adapting and aligning existing programs, some new programs were created. For instance, an overnight retreat focused specifically on competency development was established to provide a common training experience and expectation for student organization leaders. This program was born out of the desire that student leaders have a common leadership development training experience in addition to a set of longstanding student organization management trainings and mandatory meetings.

Recommendations in Hindsight

As faculty and staff embarked on the systematic realignment of leadership development on campus, there are three areas of learning that serve as hindsight recommendations that may be helpful to other institutions interested in engaging in a similar process.

Connections to High-Impact Practices.   The attempt to call attention to the interconnectedness of learning between high-impact practices (i.e., serving as a Resident Assistant who engages in a service-learning immersion experience and also takes a leadership course) was a significant goal for this initiative. By using one campus-wide leadership framework to design, position, and market all high-impact practices, students now have a pathway to explicitly connect and articulate their learning across multiple experiences.

Engaging Faculty.   To attain widespread institutional success, it was important to engage and develop buy-in from faculty members early in the process. Faculty members are vital in helping gain support from their peers. In some departments, faculty recognized this initiative as a way to communicate their unique value proposition to students, resulting in potentially increasing enrollment in their department's courses or majors.

Selecting Key Team Members.   Selecting the right people from across the institution was important to the success of the initiative. Individuals who served on any of the committees and subcommittees had enough institutional knowledge to understand campus contexts. They also were able to recognize the interconnectivity between various departments' goals and were open to learning how each department contributes to college and post-college student success.

The success of the University of Iowa's "Be Better @ Iowa" initiative relies on these three recommendations, as they have been critical for the development and implementation of this initiative campus-wide.

Conclusion

"Be Better @ Iowa" has allowed the University of Iowa to articulate intentional pathways for leadership development for all undergraduate students. In fall 2016, the first semester of "Be Better @ Iowa" implementation, 964 undergraduate students engaged in a high-impact practice (Kuh, 2008) that utilized both Seemiller's Student Leadership Competencies (Seemiller, 2013b) and the Clifton StrengthsFinder assessment (Rath, 2007) as a foundation. Student engagement with these activities has reinforced the campus-wide framework, and presented opportunities for further development of courses, programs, and services that use these two components. The coordinated effort of multiple entities across the University of Iowa has resulted in greater leverage in supporting undergraduate student leadership development, and ultimately, student success.

Note

1. Gallup®, Clifton StrengthsFinder®, StrengthsFinder®, the 34 Clifton Strengths-Finder theme names, StrengthsQuest™, and Clifton StrengthsFinder Themes® are trademarks of The Gallup Organization, Princeton, NJ. Strengths Portrait™ is a trademark of Total SDI, Carlsbad, CA.

References

Agnew, S. (2014, June 4). *Regents approve performance-based funding plan.* Retrieved from http://www.press-citizen.com/story/news/education/university-of-iowa/2014/06/04/new-funding-plan-top-regents-agenda/9951251/

Berrett, D. (2016, April 3). If skills are the new canon, are colleges teaching them? *The Chronicle of Higher Education.* Retrieved from http://chronicle.com/article/If-Skills-Are-the-New-Canon/235948?cid=at

Fabris, C. (2015, January 20). College students think they're ready for the work force. Employers aren't so sure. *The Chronicle of Higher Education.* Retrieved from http://m.chronicle.com/article/College-Students-Think/151289/?cid=at

Hansen, S. (n.d.). *Welcome from the coordinator.* Retrieved from https://studentsuccess. uiowa.edu/about-us/welcome/

Kelderman, E. (2015, March 5). Republican governors' shared goals for higher ed: Accountability and work-force preparation. *The Chronicle of Higher Education.* Retrieved from http://chronicle.com/article/Republican-Governors-Shared/228227/?cid=at

Komives, S. R., Lucas, N., & McMahon, T. R. (2013). *Exploring leadership: For college students who want to make a difference* (3rd ed.). San Francisco, CA: Jossey-Bass.

Kuh, G. D. (2008). *High-impact educational practices.* Washington, DC: Association of American Colleges and Universities.

National Association for Colleges and Employers. (2016). *Job outlook 2016: The attributes employers want to see on new college graduates' resumes.* Retrieved from http://www.naceweb.org/s11182015/employers-look-for-in-new-hires.aspx

Northouse, P. G. (2015). *Introduction to leadership concepts and practices* (3rd ed.). Los Angeles, CA: Sage.

Rath, T. (2007). *StrengthsFinder 2.0.* New York, NY: Gallup Press.

Seemiller, C. (2013a). *Jossey-Bass student leadership competencies database.* Retrieved from http://www.wiley.com/WileyCDA/Section/id-818224.html

Seemiller, C. (2013b). *The student leadership competencies guidebook.* San Francisco, CA: Jossey-Bass.

Supiano, B. (2015, November 18). When choosing a college, how should students gauge the payoff? *The Chronicle of Higher Education.* Retrieved from http://chronicle.com/article/When-Choosing-a-College-How/234242

The University of Iowa. (n.d.). *About the student success team.* Retrieved from https://studentsuccess.uiowa.edu/about-us/

KELLEY C. ASHBY *has spent 20 years of her career as a leadership educator in both academic and co-curricular arenas. She served as the senior director of Academic and Leadership Programs at the University of Iowa Pomerantz Career Center while developing and implementing the "Be Better @ Iowa" leadership initiative and currently serves as a Student Leadership Competencies consultant and trainer.*

PAUL J. MINTNER *currently serves as the associate director for leadership and service programs in the Center for Student Involvement and Leadership at the University of Iowa, and currently serves as a co-chair of the "Be Better @ Iowa Initiative."*

NEW DIRECTIONS FOR STUDENT LEADERSHIP • DOI: 10.1002/yd

Index

NEW DIRECTIONS FOR STUDENT LEADERSHIP

ORDER FORM SUBSCRIPTION AND SINGLE ISSUES

DISCOUNTED BACK ISSUES:

Use this form to receive 20% off all back issues of *New Directions for Student Leadership*.
All single issues priced at **$23.20** (normally $29.00)

TITLE	ISSUE NO.	ISBN

Call 1-800-835-6770 or see mailing instructions below. When calling, mention the promotional code JBNND to receive your discount. For a complete list of issues, please visit www.wiley.com/WileyCDA/WileyTitle/productCd-YD.html

SUBSCRIPTIONS: (1 YEAR, 4 ISSUES)

☐ New Order   ☐ Renewal

U.S.	☐ Individual: $89	☐ Institutional: $363
CANADA/MEXICO	☐ Individual: $89	☐ Institutional: $405
ALL OTHERS	☐ Individual: $113	☐ Institutional: $441

Call 1-800-835-6770 or see mailing and pricing instructions below.
Online subscriptions are available at www.onlinelibrary.wiley.com

ORDER TOTALS:

Issue / Subscription Amount: $ _____

Shipping Amount: $ _____
(for single issues only – subscription prices include shipping)

Total Amount: $ _____

SHIPPING CHARGES:	
First Item	$6.00
Each Add'l Item	$2.00

(No sales tax for U.S. subscriptions. Canadian residents, add GST for subscription orders. Individual rate subscriptions must be paid by personal check or credit card. Individual rate subscriptions may not be resold as library copies.)

BILLING & SHIPPING INFORMATION:

☐ **PAYMENT ENCLOSED:** *(U.S. check or money order only. All payments must be in U.S. dollars.)*

☐ **CREDIT CARD:** ☐ VISA ☐ MC ☐ AMEX

Card number _____ Exp. Date _____

Card Holder Name _____ Card Issue # _____

Signature _____ Day Phone _____

☐ **BILL ME:** *(U.S. institutional orders only. Purchase order required.)*

Purchase order # _____
Federal Tax ID 13559302 • GST 89102-8052

Name _____

Address _____

Phone _____ E-mail _____

Copy or detach page and send to: **John Wiley & Sons, Inc. / Jossey Bass**
PO Box 55381
Boston, MA 02205-9850

PROMO JBNND

CPSIA information can be obtained
at www.ICGtesting.com
Printed in the USA
LVHW081140151020
668841LV00007B/91

9 781119 484059